HOW TO

RUIN YOUR LIFE

P9-EGN-221

ERIC GEIGER

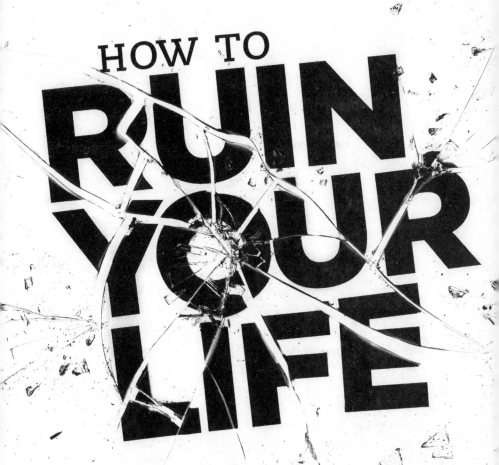

HOW TO RUIN YOUR LIFE

and Starting Over When You Do

PUBLISHING GROUP

NASHVILLE, TENNESSEE

Copyright © 2018 by Eric Geiger
All rights reserved.
Printed in the United States of America

978-1-4627-8091-4

Published by B&H Publishing Group
Nashville, Tennessee

Dewey Decimal Classification: 241
Subject Heading: CHRISTIAN ETHICS \ HUMAN BEHAVIOR \
SELF

All Scripture quotations are taken from the Christian Standard
Bible®, Copyright © 2017 by Holman Bible Publishers. Used
by permission. Christian Standard Bible® and CSB® are federally
registered trademarks of Holman Bible Publishers.

1 2 3 4 5 6 7 • 22 21 20 19 18

For my parents, Greg and Ruth Geiger, whose love and grace was always greater than my foolishness

Acknowledgments

Few people read this section but those who do should know I believe the best team in the world, in this space, the space of forming trustworthy books that can impact a person in the middle of the brokenness of this world, worked on this book. B&H, the book publishing division of LifeWay, is amazing. With all respect and admiration, thank you B&H.

Contents

Part 1: Imploded Lives

Chapter One: How to Ruin Your Life | 3

Chapter Two: If David Can | 29

Part 2: If You Want to Ruin Your Life . . .

Chapter Three: Isolate Yourself | 51

Chapter Four: Ignore Your Boredom | 73

Chapter Five: Believe in Yourself | 93

Part 3: If You Want to Start Over . . .

Chapter Six: Confess | 123

Chapter Seven: Surrender | 145

Chapter Eight: Rejoice | 159

Chapter Nine: Look to Him | 173

Notes | 177

Part 1

Imploded Lives

Chapter One

How to Ruin
Your Life

Men fall in private long before they fall in public.
—J. C. Ryle

To ruin your life, simply allow the foundation of your life to weaken. Then, toppling is inevitable.

If you ignore erosion of your integrity, you will implode. If you shrug at the explosives beneath the surface, explosives that threaten to weaken your character, you will implode. If your competence and gifting outpace your integrity, you will implode. If the weight of your responsibilities and burdens is greater than your character, you will implode. Sadly, some will stand by, watch, and cheer as you topple—and quickly move on to look for the next person they can watch fall.

Some people love to see a good implosion.

While some love the buzz and chatter a ruined life provides, implosions are devastatingly miserable for the person and horribly painful to watch in the lives of people we love. And they are too common.

Too Common

As my leadership team filled our conference room, few people spoke. It was obvious that everyone was anxious to learn why we were gathered for a meeting that had been scheduled only an hour earlier. Glances of "what in the world is going on?" were shared back and forth as people wondered what prompted this urgent and awkward meeting.

Most of our team had served alongside one another for five years, and this was only the second time an urgent meeting had been called. The previous time was when our board of trustees alerted me to anonymous communication asking them to oust me. So the team knew a meeting called so hastily meant something very somber and serious.

The team that gathered was the one responsible for leading the largest division of LifeWay Christian Resources, the ministry where we served together. We were in the middle of our most fruitful year together and the most fruitful year in the history of LifeWay, as more and more churches and individuals were being served with the resources we provided. Leadership and ministry offer ups and downs, and this year was one of the brightest years—filled with laughter, joy, and optimism about the future.

But not this meeting. This meeting was pure pain. Agonizing pain.

I mainly remember the weeping, the prayers that were uttered through tears and lumped throats, and the sharp pain of loss, disappointment, and angst all mixed together. The type of pain that stabs and cuts deep in the gut and steals every few breaths. I don't remember how I shared the news, but I could not look up as I told the team how we would not be able to continue serving with a ministry leader we all loved because of *disqualifying* behavior in the leader's life.

If only that was the only painful meeting . . .

One afternoon I received a phone call from a friend's attorney, informing me that I was in my friend's will and a check was being mailed to my house. It was a numbing phone call as my friend had recently committed suicide. Though once publicly committed to the Lord and an extremely successful businessman, his life spun out of control as he found his worth in his career. As things spiraled downward, he meticulously planned the horrible choice to end his own life, which included putting myself and others in his will. I remember him as a good man, an encourager, a man filled with wisdom.

If only that was the only painful phone call . . .

Early one morning I walked into our bedroom and my wife Kaye was crying on the phone. When she hung up, she told me that a friend of ours checked himself into a hotel and drank himself to death. In distress, his wife called to tell Kaye that his body was just discovered. His precious daughters played with my daughters many times. He was a supportive and present father, and though he loved his girls, the grip alcohol had on him was fierce.

The frequency of the stories doesn't lessen the pain of each one. Their wake seems to impact everything, even how restaurant booths feel.

Restaurant Booths

There is a restaurant in Nashville that was once one of my favorite spots for lunch. I realized one day, in the middle of a meal, that I was sitting in the same booth I sat in years earlier with a husband, father, and ministry leader I admired. His passion for the Lord was contagious. There was joy in his eyes, the kind of joy that makes some want to ask the server for whatever he is having but makes those of us who have walked with the Lord think, "this guy has spent time with Jesus today." His love for people was tangible. How he interacted with the server and others at the table was refreshing. But sitting in the same restaurant booth, reminded me how much had changed in those few years as his marriage had fallen apart and his public ministry was now over.

I looked around the restaurant and saw another booth where another leader and I once sat and dreamed about the future. We planned a project that would serve people well, prayed together, and talked about what the Lord was doing in our lives. But this leader is no longer leading either. With remorse and sadness, I looked at the booths where I previously enjoyed meals with authors and leaders I loved and respected, leaders that I felt loved Jesus more than me. Leaders who sat in those same booths are no longer serving Him in the same way. Their stories, though far from over, have taken dramatic and downward turns.

I rarely eat at that restaurant anymore. The booths are not as comfortable as they once were. Instead they surface feelings of loss, regret, and wondering what could have been different. Moments of gladness have been overshadowed by grief. Their sinful choices impacted more than just their lives as families, churches, and countless others were deeply affected. The restaurant once reminded me of pleasant conversations, and now it reminds me of painful ones, of phone calls and meetings where I have learned that people I love have been *disqualified*, at least for a season.

Disqualified. There is that word again.

Disqualified and Qualified

I could easily write about a recent story of a well-known leader, coach, college professor, or ministry leader who was removed from a position of influence because of disqualifying behavior, because of issues of character and integrity. However, the story would be old news by the time you read these words because there are always new stories as these implosions continually come to light. Competent and effective leaders in a variety of fields and disciplines forfeit their roles over deficiencies in their character. They were able to lead others but not themselves, able to grow an organization while their hearts grew cold. When a lack of integrity comes to light, leaders can be disqualified.

There is great pain in being disqualified. Maybe after submitting a resume for a job you have heard, "I am sorry. You just don't meet our qualifications." Or maybe you didn't qualify for the college you dreamed of attending. Perhaps after throwing a few deflated footballs you received a call saying, "You are disqualified from some games," and the agony of that call motivated you to go on a revenge tour all the way to the Super Bowl (Google Tom Brady if you are not qualified to understand this illustration). Regardless of the situation, being disqualified hurts.

I have been disqualified multiple times. As a child, I was disqualified in swim meets for scissor kicking instead of properly executing breaststroke. When you are disqualified, it does not matter how fast you swam, your time does not count. Your time is not even posted on the score sheet, only a "DQ" next to your name, and it doesn't mean you're getting Dairy Queen as a reward, but that you still don't know how to swim correctly despite all the practice, coaching, and lessons your parents paid for.

In elementary school some kids in my class got pulled into a new class for the "Gifted and Talented," thus leaving me behind to do normal work while they enjoyed extraordinary activities for the extraordinary kids. I appealed to my mom who appealed to the school who allowed me to take a test in an attempt to qualify myself to wear proudly the "Gifted" title. I took the extraordinary test and confidently waited a few days for the results only to have my mother come in my room one night with the words, "No matter what son, I am proud of you." I knew she was setting me up for a letdown. Turns out I was an ordinary kid and not qualified for the Gifted and Talented class.

In high school I was disqualified from representing my school at Boys State, a selective educational program for incoming seniors. After being chosen to represent our school, I was arrested with some friends after sneaking out of my house, stealing credit cards from vehicles, and driving throughout the New Orleans area, where I grew up, buying beer to sell to our friends. It was absolutely sinful and idiotic and I deserved the call that said, "You cannot represent us. You are not invited. You have been disqualified."

So I experienced disqualification because I was not good enough (failed to make Gifted and Talented) and disqualification for being bad (kicked out of Boys State). Both cut deep and are difficult to accept.

Before God, all of us were disqualified. There is a DQ next to every one of our names, next to every single one of us, from plumbers to poets to physicians to preachers. We are not nearly good enough. Even on our best days and in our brightest moments, we fall incredibly short of God's holiness. To belong to Him, one must be perfect, and we are not perfect, but terribly sinful. We have declared war against God and rebelled against His rule and reign. We don't deserve to be in His kingdom and we cannot qualify ourselves to enter it. Actually, our attempts to qualify ourselves are offensive to God because we reveal we don't believe Him to be holy or appreciate His grace. If we think we can qualify ourselves, we have mocked Him by lowering Him to our level.

But God, in His great love and grace, *qualifies* us. He does for us what we cannot do for ourselves. If you are His, if you have received His forgiveness, He has qualified you. Though you won't live perfectly today, He has declared you perfect. His perfect righteousness is now yours as all your sin was placed on Him when He sacrificed Himself on the cross on your behalf.

No matter your sin and your past, you are qualified because you are not the one who does the qualifying. He is the only One who can qualify you, and He has! The apostle Paul, in the first chapter in the book of Colossians, reminds believers in Christ of what Christ has done for us.

He has reserved us a place in heaven (Col. 1:5).

He has qualified and enabled us for an eternal inheritance (Col. 1:12).

He has rescued us from darkness (Col. 1:13).

He has transferred us into His kingdom (Col. 1:13).

He has redeemed us and forgiven us (Col. 1:14).

If His grace qualifies us, then why I am using this word "disqualified?" If He has declared those in Him as qualified, who am I, or anyone else, to make the call that someone is disqualified? Why does a character implosion disqualify? It is a good question.

Disqualified is a sharp word. It has a definite edge to it. It isn't soft or mushy or ambiguous. And though the word elicits a response, I don't use it to do so. I use it to be clear. Organizations wisely expect their leaders to be men and women of character. They intuitively understand that people won't follow leaders they don't respect and trust. In the Scripture, the Lord gives clear qualifications for leading others in the church. The overseer must be above reproach, gentle and hospitable, not greedy, lead his family well, and have a good reputation with outsiders.[1] If there are clearly defined qualifications for leading, then one can be disqualified from leading others.[2]

The *disqualified* word must not be thrown around lightly or haphazardly. It must be reserved for clear and consistent failures to exhibit the qualifications of leadership. It must not be based on rumor or conjecture. In fact, according to the Scripture, people within a local church should not accept accusations against their leaders unless multiple witnesses bring those accusations.[3] And views on a blog or "likes" on a Facebook post do not count as multiple witnesses.

One can be qualified by His grace and disqualified to lead at the same time. To be disqualified from leading in no way contradicts the beautiful reality and glorious news that His grace qualifies us.

Disqualification for issues of character is always preceded by an implosion of integrity, by a leader falling apart internally before the ruin and rubble is seen externally. In some sense, all of us are leaders—as God has given humanity the privilege of stewarding this world and influencing others. And whatever God has given us stewardship over is deeply impacted when our lives implode.

How Do You Implode?

Implosion is the opposite of explosion. In an explosion, matter and energy flow outward while in an implosion matter and energy collapse inward. When something implodes, it collapses from the inside.

Demolition experts can take buildings down from the outside. Large wrecking balls attached to cranes wreak havoc on the building and pummel it repeatedly until there is nothing left. The attack from the outside is visible to everyone and catches no one by surprise as the wrecking ball attached to a large crane announces to the world what is about to go down.

Demolition experts can also take buildings down from the inside. They can cause the building to implode. Except for the caution tape, the attack on the building is not obvious to onlookers. Everything looks normal on the surface, but inside the building a dramatic fall has been planned for weeks, even months. When the moment of implosion happens, it is fast and devastating.

I remember the first time I watched a building implode. I was a child and my father, who was an engineer, took me to a scheduled building implosion of the largest building at the chemical company where he worked. A horn sounded and in a matter of seconds, the building crumbled on top of itself. People cheered, chatted for a few moments, and then got in their cars and drove away. *Some people love to see a good implosion.*

On the way home my father explained that the implosion took weeks of planning. While the implosion appeared rapid to the onlookers who were eager to see something fall, there was an intentional weakening of the foundation through a series of strategic and sequenced explosives. Explosive devices were placed at key foundational areas in the large building. They were lit in sequence, and when the building was weakened it simply caved on top of itself. As the structure beneath the surface failed, the building could no longer hold the immense weight and ruin was inevitable.

Though the fall may seem fast to onlookers, *ruining your life does not happen overnight.*

This Book

Here is what I am *not* going to do in this book: I am not naming names. This is not a tell-all. This is not a pile-on. Not a book that takes shots at men and women I love who are wounded. While I have learned a lot from others describing their implosion, and will pass on some insights in this book, I hold on to hope for greater days for these men and women.

I am also not going to throw out a bunch of stats about the number of Christian marriages that are imploding, the number of Christians who are self-destructing though a myriad of addictions, or the number of ministry and business leaders who are walking away from their responsibilities. Those stats can be helpful in alerting us to our own fragility, but I suspect that the frequency of men and women ruining their lives already has your attention. You know this is a problem. You have friends who have ruined their lives and have read some of the same stories I have read. Some hypothesize that implosions are not any more rampant now than before, that we merely hear of them more with the constant news and continual social media feeds. Perhaps that is true. Regardless, ruined lives are too rampant.

Instead of looking at stats, we are going to look at the story of one person's implosion, David, the leader of God's people whose ruin culminated in adultery and murder. As the second king of Israel, David is an important person in history and a key figure in the story of the Bible.

David's implosion story is both instructive and inspirational. In the story we can see the explosives that weakened the foundation of his character. By looking at these, we can learn how to avoid our own self-destruction. But in David's story, we also see that God's grace is greater than our sin and our struggles. We learn that ruin does not need to be the end of our story. We can begin again.

The first half of the book looks at David's implosion. The second half of the book looks at David's confession and celebration. If your life has not yet imploded, my prayer is that the Lord will use the first half of the book to serve as a warning and the second half of the book to motivate you with His grace. If your life has imploded, my prayer is that you will walk away from the book with a helpful view of what happened to your heart and be filled with hope for your future.

No matter how big your implosion feels, it likely is not as dramatic as David's. And while he dealt with the consequences for years, God forgave him, restored him, and used him again. God is eager to forgive you, restore you, and use you too. Your implosion does not need to be the end of your story.

Is this Book for Me?

Leaders, pastors, coaches, and teachers are often the most public examples of the self-destruction that occurs when one wanders from the Lord, but they are not the only ones who have fallen and ruined their lives. And they are not the only ones who will fall and ruin their lives in the future. While their stories hit local newspapers and social media, there are thousands of others throughout the world that merit as much of our grief. When those in the public eye fall, their self-destruction is only more visible, not more common or likely.

So no matter who you are, if you are willing to look to the Bible to consider how you might find stronger foundations for your life, this book is for you.

For over twenty years, I have served as a ministry leader. While serving people in various ministry contexts, I have lived with the thrilling and the terrifying. Ministry service offers a front row seat to the mercy and grace of God in people's lives. You get to see people's lives transformed, marriages rescued, addictions overcome, and relationships restored. It is absolutely thrilling.

But serving in ministry simultaneously offers a front row seat to the terrifying brokenness in our world and in our lives. Tragedies, natural disasters, diseases, and death are regular reminders that our world longs for restoration, that things are broken here. But so are we, and humanity's brokenness manifests itself in a myriad of disastrous ways. A broken world brings about plenty of pain, but our own choices do as well.

There have been many painful phone calls. And the calls always reveal that a lot was happening beneath the surface that no one saw, a lot of things that were effectively hidden until the self-destruction was fully visible. Marriages seemingly come to a sudden end, but years of relational distance and deterioration beneath the surface come to light. Men seem to abruptly leave their families, but consistent patterns of neglecting their own souls are later revealed. Business leaders are called on

17

the carpet for shady deals and a lack of character, and years of smaller lapses in integrity are uncovered. Wives suddenly leave their husbands, but years of flirting and unhealthy conversations come to the surface.

How do people that start so well drive themselves to such ruin?

To answer to that question, we can look to David's son, Solomon, Israel's third king. The kings of Israel show us how common implosions are, and Solomon teaches us that wise men and women can live very foolishly. The Lord graciously gave Solomon his wisdom and told him that there would never be another person as wise as he was. Yet when he was old, Solomon's heart turned away from the Lord, and turned toward the gods his wives imported into their lives.[4] When our hearts turn from the Lord, they always turn toward foolishness, to things that won't satisfy and to seasons that will be filled with regret.

When our hearts turn from the Lord, we move toward implosion.

Let's Make a Plan

Chances are, if you are reading this book, you fit into one of three categories. First, you might be someone who wants to prevent an implosion. You are reading this book with hopes of navigating around treacherous paths that lie ahead for all of us. Second, you might be someone who has already imploded. The question before you is, "What do I do now?" Third, you fit into the category of a helper. Helpers are those who are leading others down the path of prevention or recovery. You are reading alongside someone who is willing to learn.

I propose, depending on which category you would classify yourself, that you make a plan. Let's agree now: *we will develop a strategy to live differently because of what we learn.*

Step 1: *Refuse to believe the lie that you are above implosion.* Whether you fit into categories one, two, or three, you will be tempted to believe, "That won't happen to me." This book is for everybody, and "everybody" means *especially you.* If David and his son, Solomon, can implode, you can too. Read with an open heart.

Step 2: *Read with a pen in your hand.* A highlighter would work too. You need to interact with what you learn. This will play a role in step three.

Step 3: *Do not read this book alone.* One of the foundational elements of biblical wisdom in the forthcoming pages is that isolation will lead to destruction. If you cannot read this book alongside others, commit to discussing what you learn with someone else.

If you will agree to formulate a reading strategy according to these three steps, I believe the Lord will do a great work in your heart. If an implosion is looming, He wants to turn your eyes to Him—the only One who can keep you from falling. If you have ruined your life, He wants to restore.

Now, let's begin our journey by looking at king David's story.

DAVID'S IMPLOSION & NEW BEGINNING

THE IMPLOSION	THE CONFRONTATION	THE CONFESSION	THE CELEBRATION
2 Samuel 11	2 Samuel 12	Psalm 51	Psalm 32

People You Need to Know in the Story

Saul (king): As a "head taller" than anyone else in Israel, Saul looked as if he should be king, and he was the king the people wanted, the first king of Israel. The people begged for a king because they wanted to be like other nations who had kings. God wanted to be their ruler, but because they kept insisting on an earthly king, God gave them Saul. He was a reckless leader who lacked integrity.

Samuel (prophet): Samuel's mother offered him to the Lord's service before he was born, and he served faithfully as prophet to God's people, Israel. He was the prophet who told the people Saul would be their king, the prophet who rebuked Saul and told him the Lord rejected him as king, and the prophet who anointed David as the next king.

David (king): The second king of Israel, David was chosen by God because he was "a man after God's heart." God took David from shepherding sheep to leading all of God's people. He was a skilled musician, songwriter, warrior, and leader. He was beloved by the people of Israel for "shepherding them with a pure heart and guiding them with skillful hands."

Nathan (prophet): Nathan was Samuel's successor as prophet to God's people, Israel. Nathan was the prophet who confronted and comforted David after his implosion. As Samuel was prophet during Saul's reign, Nathan was prophet during David's reign.

Uriah (soldier): As a solider in David's army, Uriah was faithful to his assignments and displayed loyalty to his fellow soldiers and his leaders.

Bathsheba (wife): She lived in David's kingdom and her house was close enough to the palace that David could see her from the roof of the palace as she bathed at night. Bathsheba was married to Uriah.

Joab (army general): As the general of David's military, Joab was an exceptional military strategist who guided Israel's army to many victories. Joab was loyal to David but also willing to confront him and hold him accountable for immoral and unwise actions.

Others Mentioned

Solomon (king): David's son, born to him after marrying Bathsheba, Solomon was the third king of Israel. Solomon was the wisest man to ever live and the one God chose to build the temple for Israel. He wandered from the Lord in his later years, and his kingdom split in two after his death.

Uzziah (king): As king many years after David led God's people, Uzziah was one of the kings of the Southern kingdom of Israel after the nation divided. God prospered Uzziah but when he grew prideful, his pride led to his downfall.

| THE **IMPLOSION** 2 Samuel 11 | THE **CONFRONTATION** 2 Samuel 12 | THE **CONFESSION** Psalm 51 | THE **CELEBRATION** Psalm 32 |

2 Samuel 11

In the spring when kings march out to war, David sent Joab with his officers and all Israel. They destroyed the Ammonites and besieged Rabbah, but David remained in Jerusalem. One evening David got up from his bed and strolled around on the roof of the palace. From the roof he saw a woman bathing—a very beautiful woman. So David sent someone to inquire about her, and he said, "Isn't this Bathsheba, daughter of Eliam and wife of Uriah the Hethite?" David sent messengers to get her, and when she came to him, he slept with her. Now she had just been purifying herself from her uncleanness. Afterward, she returned home. The woman conceived and sent word to inform David: "I am pregnant."

David sent orders to Joab: "Send me Uriah the Hethite." So Joab sent Uriah to David. When Uriah came to him, David asked how Joab and the troops were doing and how the war was going. Then he said to Uriah, "Go down to your house and wash your feet." So Uriah left the palace, and a gift from the king followed him. But Uriah slept at the door of the palace with all his master's servants; he did not go down to his house. When it was reported to David, "Uriah didn't go home," David questioned Uriah, "Haven't you just come from a journey? Why didn't you go home?" Uriah answered David, "The ark, Israel, and Judah are dwelling in tents, and my master Joab and his soldiers are camping in the open field. How can I enter my house to eat and drink and sleep with my wife? As surely as you live and by your life, I will not do this!" "Stay here today also," David said to Uriah, "and tomorrow I will send you back." So Uriah stayed in Jerusalem that day and the next. Then David invited Uriah to eat and drink with him, and David got him drunk. He went out in the evening to lie down on his cot with his master's servants, but he did not go home.

The next morning David wrote a letter to Joab and sent it with Uriah. In the letter he wrote: "Put Uriah at the front of the fiercest fighting, then withdraw from him so that he is struck down and dies." When Joab was besieging the city, he put Uriah in the place where he knew the best enemy soldiers were. Then the men of the city came out and attacked Joab, and some of the men from David's soldiers fell in battle; Uriah the Hethite also died. Joab sent someone to report to David all the details of the battle. He commanded the messenger, "When you've finished telling the king all the details of the battle—if the king's anger gets stirred up and he asks you, 'Why did you get so close to the city to fight? Didn't you realize they would shoot from the top of the wall? At Thebez, who struck Abimelech son of Jerubbesheth? Didn't a woman drop an upper millstone on him from the top of the wall so that he died? Why did you get so close to the wall?'—then say, 'Your servant Uriah the Hethite is dead also.'" Then the messenger left.

When he arrived, he reported to David all that Joab had sent him to tell. The messenger reported to David, "The men gained the advantage over us and came out against us in the field, but we counterattacked right up to the entrance of the city gate. However, the archers shot down on your servants from the top of the wall, and some of the king's servants died. Your servant Uriah the Hethite is also dead." David told the messenger, "Say this to Joab: 'Don't let this matter upset you because the sword devours all alike. Intensify your fight against the city and demolish it.' Encourage him."

When Uriah's wife heard that her husband Uriah had died, she mourned for him. When the time of mourning ended, David had her brought to his house. She became his wife and bore him a son. However, the Lord considered what David had done to be evil.

Chapter Two

If David Can

Whoever thinks he stands must be careful not to fall.
— 1 Corinthians 10:12

ne of the most popular business books in recent years is *Good to Great* by Jim Collins. For a season it was a must read for leaders and leadership teams. Phrases from the book became common biz-speak and were continually referenced to teach lessons from the book or impress others with business chops and prowess. Because of the book, if you said something like, "Let's get the right people on the bus, go with our hedgehog, and work for the flywheel, all while being level five leaders" many would have nodded wholeheartedly. In his work, Jim Collins provided incredible insight, based on meticulous research, on how companies that were "good" in terms of their performance became "great." Companies who did not stand out, provided modest results, and would never make any headlines, became great companies, companies that people fought to work for and other companies feared fighting. They moved from mediocrity to providing incredible value for customers and investors and rose to the top of their industries. They were great and mighty.[1]

But another book needed to be written.

In the midst of a changing market and changing times, some of the great companies slipped into mediocrity. They lost their way and struggled. For example, Circuit City, one of the companies profiled in the book, filed for Chapter 11 bankruptcy and later disappeared completely. So Jim Collins wrote another book called *How the Mighty Fall*, as some of the previously mighty companies were great no more.[2] As quickly as they had risen to be chronicled in a book about achieving greatness, they became cautionary tales. Time proved that, even while they were great, they were frail.

Great and Frail

The reality is that even incredible companies don't always make it to the next generation. And if they do survive, they often are merely surviving. Not one company will endure for all time. No matter how much cash they have in reserves, the charisma of their current leader, or how amazing their technology, no company will last forever. Only the people of God, the Church, will stand through all the changes and challenges.

All people are frail, just as all companies are frail. Not just some of us—all of us. Even those viewed as great and mighty and strong. While we should be saddened when men and women ruin their lives, we should not be surprised or shocked—even if these men and women have been stronger and godlier than we are. Implosions of great and godly men and women point to our fragility.

If there were ever a person who people believed would be above falling, above imploding, it would be David. David penned psalms, defeated a giant, defended God's people, conquered enemies, united God's people, and received God's promise that his throne would last forever (which is presently happening because Jesus Christ came into our world through the lineage of David). David was so powerful that even men around him were considered mighty. There was a time when "David's mighty men" was a thing.[3]

When we read about David, we can easily feel dwarfed by his passion for God, his skillful leadership, and his bold moves for the Lord. He was a great man, a skillful leader, a passionate worshipper, and a brilliant artist.

Yet He fell. Imploded.

The story of David's implosion jumps out in the biblical narrative and disturbs us. It jolts us because David's implosion is so out of sync with all we read about him beforehand. His implosion confronts us with the reality of our own fragility and struggles. Before we can understand the significance of the implosion, let's be sure we understand the backstory, the great years.

The Great Years

Before there was David, there was king Saul (Israel's first king). The prophet Samuel declared that God chose David to be the king of Israel—while Saul was still king of Israel—because, in David, God "found a man after His own heart."[4] The phrase is important in Israel's history because Saul was the exact opposite. Unlike David, Saul was never accused of being too passionate for the Lord. Instead, Saul was consumed with his own reputation and a king *after the people's heart.*[5]

God's people, living in the land the Lord had graciously given them, wanted a king because every other nation had a king. They rejected God as their true King to absurdly trade Him for an earthly one. Thus after their continual begging, God said, "Fine, here you go. Here is Saul." As expected, Saul proved to be an unfit and unfaithful king who disobeyed God and continually led for his own name and glory by his own strength and power. During his tenure, Saul grew colder to the Lord and more foolish in his leadership. He was consumed with jealousy and rage toward his successor, David, and his destruction culminated in a battle he lost where he disgracefully took his own life by his own sword.[6]

Even though Saul was the king the people wanted, God was gracious and gave them a new king, a better king. He gave them David.

Years before David became king, while Saul was still serving as king, God sent the prophet Samuel to the town of Bethlehem (the same one we sing about at Christmas) to the home of a man named Jesse, to anoint one of his sons as Israel's next king. Jesse marched seven sons before Samuel, but none of them were the one God appointed. One of the sons impressed Samuel, a tall and strong man who looked the part of king, but God told Samuel, "Man looks at the outward appearance, I look at the heart. He is not the one." Samuel asked Jesse if there were any others. Jesse admitted there was another son, the youngest one, the one working in the fields with sheep, the son no one would think would be the actual king. When David was brought to Samuel, God told Samuel to anoint him with oil to signify that he was the one to lead God's people.[7]

Though David knew he would be the next king, Saul was still the current king for several more years. Because Saul liked to listen to music when he was struggling with depression and anxiety, and because he heard David was a skilled musician, he invited David into his court as both a musician and warrior.

David, as he humbly waited to be king and trusted God's timing, played music for Saul.

David shattered stereotypes, as he was artist and athlete, creative and administrative, maker and manager, one of those guys who can masterfully play a recital after running through players on the opposing team. He could skillfully play music *and* beat lots of people up. His warrior ways are well chronicled from killing lions and bears, beheading a giant, and bringing foreskins of two hundred Philistines to Saul, who only asked for one hundred. With that one, we can debate which is stranger: *the ask* or David going the extra mile to exceed expectations.[8]

Regardless, David's reputation as a warrior grew greater than Saul's reputation, and Saul hated him for it. People sang songs about David's greatness: "Saul has slain his thousands and David his tens of thousands." The comparison crushed Saul because his reputation was his god, so Saul turned on David and spent years pursuing David in attempts to kill him.[9]

Though the names are different, you have probably seen this situation before. Jealousy can drive people to do really dumb things, to waste incredible amounts of time defending their own reputation by attempting to tear down someone else's. Jealousy always originates as pride, which, as we will see in the coming pages, always precedes destruction.

As David ran from Saul, he trusted God's providence and provision and worshipped the Lord while living in caves, though he knew the palace was promised. He was filled with joy, not because of his surroundings but because he delighted in the Lord and worshipped Him in the midst of the chaos. David's great years were not free from trial and turmoil. They were great because he trusted the Lord, and great because the Lord used all the pain to prepare David.

Great days are not free from turmoil, but free from our hearts growing cold and the misery and deep regret of self-destruction. Your great days may not be filled with affluence or influence, but they are filled with Him.

After Saul committed suicide, David was installed as king. The man after God's own heart replaced the man after the people's heart.

As king, David shepherded God's people well, with skillful hands and a pure heart. He united the people. He defeated enemies and secured the borders. He made Jerusalem the capital and brought the ark of the covenant to the city. Nathan, the Lord's prophet, delivered God's message to David: "I took you from tending a flock to be ruler over my people. I have been with you wherever you have gone, and I have destroyed all your enemies. I will make a great name for you like that of the greatest on earth. . . . Your house and kingdom will endure forever before me forever, and your throne will be established forever."[10]

All this was *before*, not after, the night where David's implosion culminated in deceit, destruction, and death. David was a man after God's own heart *before* the dreaded night when he ruined his life. David received the promise of God *before* he drifted into horrific disobedience. God used David in mighty and tangible ways *before* he became an adulterer, liar, and murderer.

The last chapter in the Bible immediately *before* David's fall is yet another indication of David's strength. Second Samuel 10 recounts how some of Israel's enemies "made peace with Israel and became their subjects."[11] The chapter ends with David on top of his game, with Israel thriving, and with the Lord handing another one of David's enemies to him. But when we turn the page in David's life and in the Scripture to 2 Samuel 11, we see clearly how the frail and mighty fall.

Chapter 11

The phrase *chapter 11* surfaces agonizing memories for many. When a company falls and needs to restructure because they cannot afford to operate and pay those they owe money, they can file for Chapter 11 bankruptcy protection. It is a humbling and public declaration of failure, an admission that the company has serious problems and cannot function in the same way.

David's chapter 11 filing was a public declaration of his failure to trust God and obey Him. The fallout and the consequences of David's sin were excruciatingly painful and far-reaching. And in *chapter 11* of the book of 2 Samuel we read how a man after God's own heart ruined his life:

> In the spring when kings march out to war, David sent Joab with his officers and all Israel. They destroyed the Ammonites and besieged Rabbah, but David remained in Jerusalem. One evening David got up from his bed and strolled around on the roof of the palace. From the roof he saw a woman bathing—a very beautiful woman. So David sent someone to inquire about her, and he said, "Isn't this Bathsheba, daughter of Eliam and wife of Uriah the Hethite?" David sent messengers to get her, and when she came to him, he slept with her. Now she had just been purifying herself from her uncleanness. Afterward, she returned home. The woman conceived and sent word to inform David: "I am pregnant." (2 Sam. 11:1–5)

After David learned Bathsheba was pregnant, he did not repent. Instead of allowing the news to rattle him and awaken him to the stupidity of his sin, he devised a plan to deceive her husband. Instead of owning his sin and seeking forgiveness, he sought a way to cover his tracks. In his mind, he could fix things and continue enjoying "the great years."

You've probably seen people live in self-deception and lie to themselves and others that everything is OK, that they can make things right again. Perhaps a friend struggling with an addiction assured you "I've got this," as you painfully watched his life spiral out of control. Or maybe you felt the sting of the phrase "you don't understand the pressure I am facing, I will be fine after this season passes," when you confronted someone you love on her deteriorating character. David's self-belief, his insistence that "he had this covered," only brought more ruin and destruction.

David sent for Bathsheba's husband, Uriah, who was bravely fighting for David and Israel. Uriah came to the palace where David engaged in small talk: "Tell me how the men are doing? Do you have enough resources? Do you miss your family?"

Perhaps Uriah wondered why David was not on the battlefield as he had been before, but there is no way he asked. No way he would have asked the king such a pointed and potentially offensive question. Of course David assumed when he inquired about Uriah's wife, the woman who had recently spent the night in the palace where they talked, that Uriah's desire would drive him home to his wife. But Uriah exhibited much more self-control than David, and did not go home. He could not bring himself to do so when men he fought alongside were sleeping on the ground away from their loved ones. No, Uriah slept at the door of the palace. David's plan for a cover-up was thwarted by the pure loyalty of Uriah to the men he fought alongside.

When David discovered that his plan failed, he did not give up. David invited Uriah over a second night for dinner and drinks. As David got Uriah drunk, as he saw him slurring his words and speaking more freely, he surely thought, "Got him. With his senses numbed and his inhibitions lowered, he will go to his wife and my sin will be covered." Only Uriah did not go home. Once again, he slept outside of his home.

David's next move revealed how calloused and cold his heart had grown. He sunk even deeper into sin, did the unthinkable, and became the man he swore he would never be. Just as Saul had misused power and military resources to chase David across the countryside, David devised a scheme to misuse his military resources to have Uriah killed. The man after God's own heart became a murderer. The man who passionately worshipped the God of Light and Life sunk deeper into darkness and became an instrument of death.

David knew he could trust Uriah with instructions. After all, Uriah was the man who would not even go home to his own wife because of loyalty to the king, to the mission, and to his fellow soldiers. David crafted a letter to Joab, his military general, and sent it with Uriah. Uriah did not realize he was carrying his own death certificate as the letter contained instructions to "put Uriah at the front of the fiercest fighting, then withdraw from him so that he is struck down and dies."[12] David ordered the execution of one of his own men, one who in his blind loyalty, never considered peering into the letter he carried ordering his own death. There has not been a Netflix original or Dateline special more scandalous than this story.

David breathed a sigh of relief when Joab sent word back that Uriah was dead. In his mind, his sin was erased. Out of sight and, hopefully soon, out of mind. Sure, David felt guilty. But he reasoned that he could move on past his guilt eventually. After all, people die in battle all the time, so was this *really* that bad? And move on, David did.

> Bathsheba mourned the loss of her husband and when
> the time of her mourning ended, David brought her to
> his house. She became his wife and bore him a son.
> (2 Sam. 11:27)

As Bathsheba moved into the palace, David believed he had covered his own sin. It was messy. It was a lot of work. But his elaborate plan worked and it was time to continue with life. He had a new wife and a new son to care for. Uriah was sacrificed, unwillingly and unknowingly, so David could continue to live the glory years.

Yet chapter 11 ends with a sobering statement: "However, the Lord considered what David had done to be evil."[13]

The Lord saw all of it. The Lord watched as David's heart grew cold, as David stopped pursuing Him and pursued a married woman instead. Sin always makes us stupid, always numbs our senses, and the Lord watched as David's lust drove him to foolishness. The Lord saw David's attempt at a lavish cover-up, from David calling Uriah home to David writing the letter that would lead to Uriah's death.

Because the Lord sees everything, our attempts to hide our own sins always fail. And with David, God chose discipline that was both painful and public.

Consequences Remain

When a man leaves his wife for another lover, forgiveness from the Lord is available. But his children's view of marriage is altered, the way they look at him is changed, and holidays are a regular reminder that consequences remain.

When a woman neglects her family for her career, forgiveness is free and abundant when she turns to the Lord, but the pain she caused her family can remain and the regret she has does not easily go away.

When an employee, longing to climb the corporate ladder, lies and manipulates his way into an open position, forgiveness is free, but the lack of integrity will cost him as he looks for new jobs.

A friend of mine from high school is in prison for the rest of his life for murder. He has confessed faith in Christ, received forgiveness, and the Lord sees him as pure and perfect because Christ is his Savior. But as he woke up this morning in a jail cell, the consequences in this life remain.

God sent a prophet named Nathan to confront David in his sin. Like any good preacher, Nathan set up David with a killer illustration: "David, there were two men in a certain city. One was filthy rich. He had tons of cattle, tons of sheep, lots of money, and could afford anything he wants. The other guy was poor. He only had one lamb and he loved it. He treated the lamb like a daughter, fed the lamb from his own plate and even snuggled with it. One day the rich man had a guest visit and instead of slaughtering one of his many animals, he killed the poor man's lamb for his dinner party."[14]

When David heard the story, he burned with anger. As king, he would not tolerate that type of ridiculous and self-ish and evil behavior in one of the cities under his watch. He wanted justice and restitution, so he fiercely declared: "As the Lord lives, the man who did this deserves to die! Because he has done this thing and shown no pity, he must pay four lambs for that lamb."[15] David's sense of justice was incredibly ironic.

David missed the point of the illustration. In his blindness, he was angered by another's sin while being hardened to his own.

We are often the same way. We can be exponentially more disgusted with the sin in other people's lives than we are with the sin in our own. Our own sin can fail to anger us the way someone else's sin does.

"You are the man!" Nathan replied.[16]

You are the man! Guys will sometimes use that phrase with each other after a good play on the court, after a good performance on the job, or when hearing that one of their buddies has landed a first date. Guys typically enjoy hearing the sound of that phrase, but not this time. This time the phrase stung deeply. "David, you are the one who has done this evil. And the Lord's message for you is this: You did this evil *after* I anointed you as king, *after* I rescued you from Saul, *after* I gave you the palace and the throne. I was good and gracious to you, yet you despised me and did this evil. Because you despised me, the sword will never leave your house and I am going to bring disaster on you and your family. You did this in secret, but your discipline will be in public."

Just as God's promise to David that his kingdom would never end has been fulfilled in Christ, God's promise to David about the consequences of his sin were also fulfilled. The son he had with Bathsheba died as an infant. One of his sons, Absalom, murdered another one of his sons, Amnon. Absalom publicly humiliated David by pursuing the crown and planning his father's assassination. When Absalom was brutally killed, David mourned bitterly, "My son Absalom! My son, my son Absalom! If only I had died instead of you, Absalom, my son, my son!"[17]

David knew that the strife and struggles he faced through the rest of his life were because of the Lord's discipline for his sin. One day, when he was publicly mocked and his men wanted to kill the mocker, David replied, "The Lord told him to do it."[18] David was keenly aware that his sin had far-reaching consequences. He was forgiven, but he lived with the consequences of his sin for the rest of his life. His sin was erased but the consequences in this life were not.

Consequences often remain even after forgiveness has been received.

What Went Wrong?

We should be grateful that the story of David's implosion is in Scripture. The story reminds us that none of us are above ruining our lives and that even when we do God's grace is greater than our sin. The story also teaches us how to avoid the implosion. David's story provides insight on how exactly we can ruin our lives *so that* we can avoid ruining our lives. The story instructively helps us see what was really going wrong in David's heart. Not only did God see David's actions, but He also saw his heart. And in the first several verses of chapter 11, Scripture gives us a peek into David's heart, into what was happening internally that would lead to such a great fall externally.

Just as demolition experts place explosives inside of buildings so they will weaken and implode, there were three explosives on the foundation of David's life that led to his implosion. These three explosives can lead to your ruin as well. They are easily hidden from those who watch us from a distance, but they threaten to destroy the foundation of our lives.

The three explosives are *isolation*, *boredom*, and *pride*.

Read again the first four verses of chapter 11 and look for isolation, boredom, and pride.

> In the spring when kings march out to war, David sent
> Joab with his officers and all Israel. They destroyed the
> Ammonites and besieged Rabbah, but David remained
> in Jerusalem. One evening David got up from his bed
> and strolled around on the roof of the palace. From
> the roof he saw a woman bathing—a very beautiful
> woman. So David sent someone to inquire about her,
> and he said, "Isn't this Bathsheba, daughter of Eliam
> and wife of Uriah the Hethite?" David sent messengers
> to get her, and when she came to him, he slept with
> her. (2 Sam. 11:1–4)

First, David was *alone*. He was isolated. It was the time that kings go off to war, and David remained in Jerusalem. He sent his community away. Friends who would have held him accountable were gone. Friends who would have stopped him from pursuing Bathsheba were nowhere around.

Second, David was *bored*. He got up from his bed in the middle of the night looking for something, anything. The Lord, on that night, was not enough for Him. He wanted something else, something else to look at, something else to conquer, something else to pursue.

Third, David was filled with *pride*. When he was told that Bathsheba was Uriah's wife, David instructed the servant to get her anyway. "I am the king and I get what I want." In his mind, David deserved whatever he desired. Pride corrupted his heart.

Isolation. Boredom. Pride. They must not be taken lightly. They will ruin a life. We will talk about these in the next several chapters, but here is a simple preview on how to ruin your life:

1. Isolate yourself.
2. Ignore your boredom.
3. Believe in yourself.

How the Mighty Fall

Jim Collins is not the only one to use the phrase "how the mighty fall." Sports announcers have used it to describe athletes who were rich and lost everything. People in the marketplace have used the phrase to depict business leaders who made it to the top of the corporate ladder only to plunge after a few bad quarters. And Jim Collins was also not the first person to use the phrase.

David coined the phrase.

As Saul's self-destruction culminated with his brutal death at his own hand, David mourned by lamenting, "How the mighty have fallen!"[19] David actually put the phrase into a song he wrote about Saul's demise. Before David ruined his life, he crafted and created a song about how a life can be ruined. David watched what happens when a person cares more about success than sanctification, more about reputation than character. David watched the pride in Saul's life grow like a cancer and lead him further and further from the Lord. David saw the tragedy of the implosion and understood the fragility of the human heart and the destruction that happens when we are in awe of ourselves instead of in awe of God.

Yet a night came when the man who wrote and sang the phrase "How the Mighty Have Fallen" was unable to keep himself from falling because he was no longer focused on the only One who could.

Isolation, boredom, and pride are not sins to tame, but sins that must be slain. They lead to a myriad of other sins and ultimately to self-destruction. We must not ignore them, and we are wise to learn how to overcome them.

Part 2

If You Want to Ruin Your Life . . .

Chapter Three

Isolate Yourself

> *Sin demands to have a man by himself.*
> — *Dietrich Bonhoeffer*

For more than fifteen years, you have likely been exposed to ads with the messaging, "If you see something, say something." An ad agency developed the campaign shortly after the horrific terrorist attacks of September 11, 2001. They created posters featuring a picture of an unattended bag on a subway car with the messaging, "If you see something, say something. Be suspicious of anything unattended." While some federal agencies initially rejected the campaign, the NYC Transportation Authority adopted it to encourage residents and tourists to report any suspicious behavior. As reports rose in New York, others organizations and agencies started using the phrase. You have likely heard it in airports, theme parks, or other places where large crowds gather.[1]

The messaging was clear and catalyzed people to be more alert and report suspicious behavior, to look for anything that is unattended. After all, the stakes were and are too high to not "say something if you see something."

The same is true in Christian community. Being in community with others who love and fear God means being confronted and confronting. We live, work, and worship alongside broken and struggling brothers and sisters. And all of us, no matter how long we have walked with the Lord, are recovering from our own issues.

All of us are prone to wander and fall, so we need people around us who "say something if they see something." We need people around us who love us enough to confront us when our hearts are unattended by truth, when our relationships are unattended by forgiveness, and when our decisions are unattended by the Lord's agenda.

To set yourself up for an implosion, simply fail to surround yourself with people who will say something to you when they see your life unattended. To implode, choose isolation over community.

To set up your family or friends for implosion, cower and remain silent when you see something suspicious in their lives. Don't speak up; don't say anything. To help them to implode, enable isolation by looking the other way.

When David ruined his life, he was living in isolation. Those who would have said something, who would have held him accountable, who would have refused to execute his plan to pursue a married woman, were gone. David had sent them away. They were at war. They were where he belonged. The chapter that chronicled David's fall begins with clear clues that something is about to go terribly wrong.

> In the spring when kings march out to war, David sent Joab with his officers and all Israel. They destroyed the Ammonites and besieged Rabbah, but David remained in Jerusalem. (2 Sam. 11:1)

During the season when kings typically marched out to war with their men, David remained in Jerusalem, his home city where his palace was located. Not only did David stay behind, but he also sent Joab and other leaders away. He sent away community and embraced isolation. And a few verses later, we see the devastating result of isolation in David's adultery.

Why does it matter that David was alone without Joab and the others? How do we know that Joab would have said something if he saw something?

Joab was Israel's military commander and he served alongside David for decades. We learn later that Joab, though far from perfect, was willing to confront and challenge David when David's heart drifted, when his life was unattended by

God's greatness and grace. One thing we can conclude about Joab: he was not guilty of enabling isolation.

One time, later in David's life, David fell to temptation and ordered all in his kingdom counted. He placed Joab in charge of the census to learn just how strong Israel was. David's decision to count the troops indicated that David's security was in his army and not his Lord. David also disobeyed how a census should be taken.[2] The Lord had been clear, that each person counted was to give to the temple, but David disregarded the Lord's command, hastily ordered the census, and brought judgment on the people as his actions "were evil in God's sight." In the midst of the sin surrounding the census, Joab confronted David, asked him why he would do such an evil thing, and did not fully obey David's orders to count all of the people because the "kings command was too detestable to him." Joab was willing to stand up to David, to say something when he saw David's heart drift.[3]

On another occasion, Joab confronted David for not loving his troops well, and even told David "he shamed himself and all the soldiers." Joab pushed through the bubble that David attempted to create around himself and challenged David to love those he led. Because Joab wanted David to thrive as king, Joab risked the uneasiness of confronting his boss.

But Joab was not with David when David pursued a married woman.

When David chose isolation over community, the man who would challenge and correct him was off fighting. Joab was one of the few people in David's life who was not overly impressed with David, who was willing to tell him the truth and remind him of the Lord's commands. With people like Joab sent away from David, all that remained were people who were in awe of him, people who shook in his presence, people who would quickly bring the wife of another man to him.

The lure of isolation on David's heart was strong—and it ruined him.

The Lure of Isolation

Isolation is often very attractive, and it is on the rise with no signs of slowing down. Nearly twenty years ago Robert Putnam wrote a landmark book called *Bowling Alone* because his research revealed that bowling leagues, among other opportunities for connection and relationships, were declining. Yet bowling was not declining. In fact, the number of bowlers over a twenty-year period of time *increased* while the number of people in bowling leagues greatly *decreased*. Instead of bowling in community, people were bowling alone. Putnam warned that the move toward isolation would ultimately hurt people and communities.[4]

Putnam issued his warning about isolation before restaurant booths would be filled with people staring at their iPhones instead of connecting with each other, before binge-watching Netflix would become common in our culture, and before social media was invented, much less classified as an addiction. The move to isolation only gets easier, and thus more common. Our drive for individualism and our longing to escape make isolating ourselves very tempting.

Individualism

David, in his mind, had many reasons to rely on his strength as a great leader and man, to insist that he could stand on his own. His approval ratings among the people were strong and his resume was impressive. People regularly affirmed him and former enemies bowed before him. He likely thought, "Do I really need anyone around me? Do I really need any help?"

We live in an individualistic society where the strong prove they are strong by standing alone, by not needing anyone else, and by achieving their independent status with their genius or grit. As an example, Jesse Ventura, former Navy Seal, professional wrestler, and governor of Minnesota, ridiculed the desire for Christian community when he declared, "Organized religion is a sham and a crutch for weak-minded people who need strength in numbers. It tells people to go out and stick their noses in other people's business."[5]

The values of this world encourage us to be strong, to not require help from anyone, and to achieve and accomplish. The Christian faith is very different, diametrically opposed to the thinking of this world.

Jesse Ventura is right: we are weak.

Everyone is.

Even Navy seals, professional wrestlers, and governors. As Christians, we have embraced our weakness and joyfully quit our futile attempts to achieve forgiveness so we may gratefully receive God's grace and forgiveness.

Our faith is a receiving faith, not an achieving faith. Our faith is also, because we rejoice in our weakness, not an individualistic faith. We need each other. The Christian faith is not an independent faith but an interdependent one, a faith that relies on other believers for encouragement, care, prayer, forgiveness, and support. Yet because we are affirmed for our ability to stand alone and encouraged, "you be you," there is a constant pull away from community and toward independence.

We must recognize that we are often encouraged to live in a way that can destroy us. Typically encouragements to engage in anything that could possibly harm you must be accompanied by full-disclosure statements about the potential side effects. You have heard the happy voice on commercials saying things like, "Consult your doctor before taking because side effects can be constant nausea, random rashes over your whole body, and perpetual irritability." Sign me up! But because independence is so baked into our cultural values, few voices express caution over isolation. Few voices sound the alarm to the pitfalls of not being surrounded by people who will hold us accountable.

A voice that challenged me in this area came from a friend, Steve Graves. Steve is an executive coach, author, and consultant who provides counsel from a Christ-honoring perspective. In his spare time, Steve leads a Bible study for a group of highly successful people who have imploded, a group of "used-to-bes" who are starting over and finding encouragement and grace from one another. What is a "used-to-be"? One guy "used to be" the CEO of a company until his addiction became public, another "used to be" a successful entrepreneur until he lost trust from colleagues and clients because of his lifestyle, and the list goes on and on.

Steve shared with me common themes he has seen in those who have fallen. One of most dominant themes is independence, the belief that others are unnecessary. As these successful people rose higher in their careers, they translated commonly-heralded messages about "it being lonely at the top" to mean, "no one understands me or gets me." As they grew more independent, they simultaneously grew more susceptible to ruin. Because the "used-to-bes" have learned the result of being isolated, they now wisely gather in community.

As independence grows so grows the likelihood of falling. Independence is not a sign of maturity or success but a warning sign of a looming implosion. Independence can lure us into being isolated, but so can the desire to escape.

Escapism

The desire to numb our pain can also pull us to isolation. Because the world is filled with such strife and struggles, there is a constant temptation to run away from it all. We can easily reason that being alone will help us avoid pain and pressure and the people that cause both. When betrayed and hurting, being vulnerable in community feels dangerous and being alone feels safe. When overwhelmed with the burdens of today, avoiding people gives the perception that no more burdens will be added.

The binge-watching trend points to the longing to escape. Deloitte, a consulting group, discovered that 70 percent of US consumers binge watch television shows.[6] One study revealed that those struggling with depression often use marathon-viewing sessions as attempts to move away from their negative emotions.[7] You can lose yourself for hours in the dramatic political world of the D.C. beltway or travel back in time to the 1950s and watch British royalty unfold. Netflix has effectively crafted their system to hook binge watchers, maybe even help to create more of them. Viewers don't "opt in" to continue watching the next episode. Instead you only have a few seconds to "opt out," as the show begins. You have to choose consciously *not* to be a binge watcher or you will become one by default.

Not all binge-watching is bad. Watching with a friend or spouse with carryout from a favorite restaurant can be enjoyable and relaxing (my wife and I often do on Friday nights . . . party animals that we are). Watching for enjoyment is very different than watching for an escape. While binge-watching may subtly promise an escape from reality, even for just a few hours, reality always awaits when the "stop" button is finally pressed.

Isolation may seem like a great solution to combat the pain and betrayal of this world, but it creates more struggles as it hardens our hearts. Isolation is more risky than the struggles of living in community. Yes, there are risks to being in relationships with others. Because all people are messy and imperfect, relationships will inevitably mean betrayal, being taken advantage of, being letdown, or being misquoted and misunderstood. But the risk of being in isolation is much greater.

The Cure of Community

Another reason community is a challenge and isolation is appealing is that community can just be awkward. For years I have encouraged people to get into a small group or Bible study at their church because I know that being in a group will have a tremendous impact on their growth as Christians. I was once a part of a huge research project, and we discovered that those who are in a group that studies the Bible show attributes of being a disciple of Jesus much more so than those who are not in a group.[8] I have preached community and will continue to preach it, but I know how uncomfortable and weird going to an organized group can be. I have seen people wince at the idea of getting in a group, of being known by a new group of people they don't yet know.

The wincing is not unfounded. There have been plenty of awkward group experiences. There is the random person that finds any opportunity in the Bible study to surface politics or the end of the world. There is the person who never talks but always stares—the really long piercing stares. There is the person who unloads all their problems—and there are many—on the very first meeting with a dominating monologue that becomes the centerpiece of the whole night.

Yet when people stick with community, a beautiful thing happens. The man obsessed with politics starts talking about the kingdom of God more and about earthly kingdoms less. The person who initially only stared through people begins to open up and share incredible insight, and everyone learns that there was beauty and thoughtfulness and love beneath the staring. And the person who unloaded all their problems is the person who is there for you when your crisis hits, who brings you dinner, sends encouraging messages, and picks your kids up from school.

Community is beautifully awkward and awkwardly beautiful. Sadly many people don't push through the awkwardness to get to the good stuff.

The awkwardness is even intentional in God's design, as community is often supposed to be uncomfortable. It isn't always comfortable to be confronted. It isn't always comfortable to be challenged. It isn't always comfortable to learn.

God uses community to mature His people, and the means for maturing are often uncomfortable. Think about it: most of the things that mature you are uncomfortable. From trials to breaking out of your comfort zone and trying something new—those seasons of growth produce growth in you.

The writer of Hebrews reminds us to "encourage each other daily, while it is still called today, so that none of you is hardened by sin's deception."⁹ Encouragement from other Christ-followers is what God uses to keep our hearts from hardening. Community is what keeps us from self-deception and in the faith. God uses community to keep His people for Himself.¹⁰

With David, God used community to bring David back to Himself. David repented because Nathan, the prophet, challenged him. David saw the stupidity and offensiveness of his sin because Nathan loved him well and cared enough to confront him, to say something when he saw something.

In isolation, David fell. In community, he repented.

When David sent Joab away, he quickly imploded. When he welcomed Nathan, he quickly repented. In isolation, David walked in darkness. In community, he walked back into the light. Nathan's loving confrontation shepherded David away from the darkness he had been living in.

Leaving the Darkness

Researchers from the University of Toronto conducted a series of experiments to discover the impact of darkness on a person's behavior. In one experiment, the researchers placed participants in two different rooms, one dark room and one filled with light, and instructed them to complete math problems and reward themselves with allotted money each time they scored correctly. Participants in both rooms performed the same on the math problems, but participants in the darker room cheated more and took money they did not earn. The darker room gave the sense of anonymity and dramatically increased cheating and lying. The researchers concluded that when people think their actions are not seen by others, when darkness gives the illusion of being isolated, people are much more likely to engage in unethical behavior.[11]

Of the relationship between spiritual darkness and isolation, Dietrich Bonhoeffer wrote:

> Sin demands to have a man by himself. It withdraws him from the community. The more isolated a person is, the more destructive will be the power of sin over him, and the more deeply he becomes involved in it, the more disastrous is his isolation. Sin wants to remain unknown. It shuns the light. In the darkness of the unexpressed it poisons the whole being of a person.[12]

Jesus invites us to walk in the light as He is in the light, to leave the darkness of our sin. But we won't walk in the light alone. The Scripture connects walking in the light with having fellowship with other believers, walking in holiness with living in community.[13] A drift from Christian community is an inevitable drift into darkness. A step away from community is a step toward implosion.

Walking in the light while living in community is much different than being in a crowd. We can be in a crowd and remain in darkness and isolation.

Alone in a Crowd

David was isolated in a crowd. Though he was not physically alone, he was isolated from those who would have cared for him and held him accountable. He was spiritually alone while surrounded by people.

If you have ever lived in a large city, you know the possibility of being alone in a crowd. Seas of people busily jam into crowded subway cars flying in one direction or sit side by side on the interstate as they commute to work. People are surrounded by others, but those that surround them are not there to carry their burden, not there to offer grace and encouragement.

People are alone among others all the time. Even with lots of "friends" on Facebook, while living in close proximity to neighbors, and while sitting in the same church, people can live isolated.

The *New York Times* published Hal Niedzviecki's experiment with his Facebook friends as proof that the word "friend" has lost meaning in our culture.[14] Hal wondered how many of his online friends were really friends, the "show up when you need them" type of friends. You know, *friend* friends. Like the real old fashioned kind. Hal wanted to gather his "friends," get to know them better, and perhaps connect them with each other. So he posted an invitation on Facebook to all seven hundred of his friends to attend a party. Fifteen people responded they "would attend" and sixty responded that "maybe they would attend." One person actually showed up. One out of seven hundred.

A much more saddening and shocking example happened on Christmas Day 2014, when some neighbors in a small town in Illinois were surprised to discover that one of their neighbors, Sunatha Simmons, had died.[15] They were more surprised to discover that she had been dead in her home for more than year. Her family came to visit from Japan and found her body in the garage. According to the coroner, she died of natural causes. More than a year and no one knew!

She should not have gone unnoticed. Her husband had passed away years earlier, and she admitted that she struggled with depression. There were even signs with her house that something was not right. Her front porch was unattended, littered with boxes, and her front yard was overgrown with weeds. You have to wonder, "What were the neighbors thinking? Did no one care enough to check on her?"

It is possible to have seven hundred social media friends without many true friends, to live in a neighborhood without having real neighbors, and to be isolated among a crowd of people.

Sunatha was associated with her neighbors in that they shared the same electric company, lived on the same street, experienced the same weather, and could watch the same local news. But clearly, association alone fails to provide care and encouragement. You can associate with people from work, church, and school and not be known, cared for, or encouraged.

Christian community implies participation, not merely association. The word in the Bible that is often translated as "fellowship" is the Greek word *koinonia*, and it carries the meaning of participation and partnership.[16] To avoid isolation, you must do more than associate; you must participate with people who will confront you and allow you to confront them. If you settle for association, you are really choosing isolation with the mere appearance of community. God desires that His people care for one another, serve one another, love one another, and encourage one another, not merely associate with one another.

Faux community is as dangerous as isolation. David associated with those in the palace who were there the night he imploded. They ate from the same kitchen, saw each other in the same hallways, and looked over the same city. David was alone in a crowd because he was surrounded by people who worked for him, not people who cared about the work of God in him.

You Are Alone in a Crowd If . . .

If you are never confronted, you are really in isolation. You have only surrounded yourself with people who are afraid of you and thus you are never challenged on your blind spots or sin. And we all have blind spots and sin. A life without confrontation is a life without growth. To live without ever being challenged is to live recklessly and spiral toward self-destruction.

If God's grace is never offered to you, you are really in isolation. Just as we all need to be confronted, we all need His grace. His grace is greater than our sin, and it is His grace that will melt our hearts and motivate us to live for Him. If people are not reminding you of God's grace offered to you in Christ, you are living in isolation.

If you are never uncomfortable, you are really in isolation. You have surrounded yourself only with people who are just like you, and you are missing the uncomfortable yet beautiful benefits of community that matures. Christian community is community that is built on Christ and not lesser common bonds. Thus Christian community pulls together people who are different than one another and are united by His grace. Those differences will cause discomfort, and the discomfort will cause growth.

If you never hear the word "No," you are really in isolation. No one should only and always hear "yes," because no one is perfect. If you have built a life for yourself where you only hear affirmations and only hear "yes," you have chosen shallow community and are surrounded with people who will passively watch you ruin your life.

If you don't give yourself to the community, you are really in isolation. Christian community is an incredible privilege and an incredible responsibility. If you don't give yourself to the community, you are playing on the fringes and grabbing the illusion of community while really remaining in isolation. If you aren't encouraging, serving, forgiving, and praying for others, you are in the darkness of isolation.

If you never weep for others, you are really in isolation. When you are in community, you love those with whom you are in community. As the trials of this world plagues others, you weep. You weep with those who weep and rejoice with those who rejoice. If you never weep, you are going through the motions and really living in isolation.

Are you alone in a crowd?

If not, thank the Lord for the community He has surrounded you with. It is not perfect, but it is good. It may be awkward at times, but it is beautifully so. If you are in isolation, throw yourself fully into the only community that will last forever—His church. Push through the awkwardness of getting deeply connected to a church, a gathering of Christ-followers, so you can get to the good stuff.

The Beauty of Christian Community

You don't have to be a Christian to understand that isolation is destructive, and you don't have to be a Christian to long for community. While we are tempted to isolate ourselves, God has wired us for community. People from a plethora of fields and backgrounds encourage and celebrate community. Parents and teachers encourage children and teenagers to get involved in extracurricular sports or activities, and online discussion groups exist for parents who struggle with a "loner child." CrossFit, the fitness regime you have likely been evangelized to join, has been compared to a church as people from all walks of life gather in their local "box" to complete the workout of the day.[17] In the midst of a digital revolution where even non-techie grandmas are jumping on social media to consume and share an insane amount of memes with cats in them, board games have made a surprising comeback. As electronic gaming becomes more impressive and more detailed, some are opting for board games again as they provide an excuse for conversations and connecting.[18]

As great as school clubs, CrossFit, and board games can be, they pale in comparison to the church. The church is not perfect, but she is beautiful. Scripture calls the church the bride of Christ, robed in His perfect righteousness. We are His, not because of anything we have done, but only because Christ pursued us and purchased us through His life and death. The early church father, Augustine, beautifully compared the first human relationship, Adam and Eve, to the church's relationship with Christ.

> When Adam was asleep, a rib was drawn from him and Eve was created; so also while the Lord slept on the Cross, His side was transfixed with a spear, and the Church was born. For the Church, the Lord's Bride, was created from His side, as Eve was created from the side of Adam. But as she was made from his side while he was sleeping, the Church was created from His side while He was dying.[19]

There is no community like the church anywhere. No other community is as transformational because no other community is formed on Christ. While people connecting around a board game or a workout of the day is a good thing and points to God's gift of relationships, people connecting around Christ is what changes, not merely comforts, the human heart.

Enjoy the beautiful awkwardness of Christian community. Embrace the risks knowing that the risks of isolation are much greater. To avoid ruining your life, come of out the darkness of isolation.

Isolation was not the only explosive in David's life that led to his downfall. He was also ruined by his own boredom, as we will see in the next chapter.

Chapter Four

Ignore Your Boredom

Sin is always, in some sense, a life of boredom.
— Martyn Lloyd-Jones

itting with an older man, a man I love and respect, I asked him about the dark period in his life—the period when he abandoned the wife of his youth for another woman. He realized the folly of his ways, repented, came home to his wife, and she graciously and fully forgave him. There was, of course, struggle and regret before the beauty of the restoration, but they are happily married now and have counseled many other couples through a similar period of darkness and strife.

"So was your marriage rocky leading up to your affair?" I asked and expected to hear of challenging times, years of distance, or a hardening of his heart toward his wife.

"No. She was great. The affair didn't begin with my marriage," he responded.

"What was it then?"

"I was bored with work, bored with my life. I was just bored."

Though boredom can sound innocent, boredom can ruin us. Boredom can tempt us to search for things we never thought we would search for and pull us in directions we never thought we would go. It can cause an unholy discontent with the lives the Lord has given, the season He has put us in. After watching numerous implosions, boredom is no longer something I view as a harmless season someone is experiencing. I cannot shrug when someone says, "It's OK. I am just bored in my life right now."

Boredom is too destructive to dismiss. One study of teenagers living in South Africa concluded that boredom is the biggest predictor of alcohol and drug abuse.[1] Parents, school counselors, and teachers are aware that "adolescent boredom" can lead to a myriad of problems, which is why many are concerned when children or students "are not challenged enough." There have even been shocking stories in recent years of people committing heinous acts in their boredom. In 2013 three teenagers in Oklahoma gunned down a college baseball player who was jogging because "they were bored and didn't have anything to do, so they decided to kill somebody."[2] Between 2003 and 2005, a German nurse killed more than thirty patients because he was "bored with his job." To give himself a challenge, he injected patients with medications that would produce fatal cardiovascular effects so he could try and resuscitate them. If the first resuscitation proved successful, he would often inject a second time to further test his abilities. All because he was bored![3]

David was bored too.

David was restless and could not sleep, so he got up from his bed and strolled around on the roof of the palace. He was uneasy and looking for something, perhaps something to conquer or something to bring him comfort. When he saw Bathsheba and was in awe of her beauty, he felt he had to have her. His boredom pulled him from his bed, drove him to a late night walk in search of something, and urged him to invite a married woman into his palace and into his arms.

An Un-bored David

But David was not always bored. There was a time, before the scandalous affair, when God was enough for him, when his awe for the Lord kept boredom from creeping into his heart. There was a time before boredom settled in his soul when God was his refuge, when God was where he set his eyes, when God was where he put his trust.

There are 150 Psalms in the Bible, written over several hundred years. They are not in chronological order but grouped by theme. Because David wrote many of them, we have a snapshot of his personal prayer journal. Let's look at entries marked

Psalm 57, Psalm 34, and Psalm 52, all written before the implosion, to see what David was praying when he was not bored with his life.

Psalm 57

While waiting to be king and hiding in a cave from the madman Saul who was attempting to kill him, David prayed, "Be gracious to me, God, be gracious to me for I take refuge in you."[4] The cave was where David hid and slept, but he declared that the Lord was his real hiding place, his ultimate refuge. It was not the only time David proclaimed God to be his refuge. In both Psalm 7 and Psalm 11, also penned by David before his implosion, David called God his refuge, the One he ran to for comfort and security.

But not the night on the roof. God was not his refuge when he saw Bathsheba bathing. God was not where he ran when he faced the pressures of being king, when he was uneasy and restless. God was not his comfort and security when he got up from his bed and searched for something else. The man who declared God to be his refuge and encouraged others to find their refuge in God sought refuge in the arms of Bathsheba.

Psalm 34

David also wrote Psalm 34 before he became king, before he was in the palace, and before he was on the roof. He penned, "those who look to Him are radiant with joy, their faces will not be ashamed."[5] He encouraged others to "turn away from evil and do what is good; seek peace and pursue it." As he looked to the Lord, he was filled with joy and was satisfied. As he turned his eyes toward the Lord, he turned his eyes from evil.

But not the night on the roof. God was not where he set his gaze. On that night, he was not looking at the Lord and finding joy in Him. His eyes were not captivated with the glory and beauty of God but with the beauty of a woman. As he turned his eyes from the Lord, he turned his eyes toward evil, toward the lust that consumed him for Bathsheba.

Psalm 52

David also wrote Psalm 52 while Saul was still on the throne. In the Psalm he wrote of his commitment to the Lord and of the reckless behavior he observed in others. He observed how another "would not make God his refuge" but instead took refuge in "the abundance of his riches" and "destructive behavior."[6] David insisted "in the presence of the faithful people, I will put hope in your name."[7]

But not the night on the roof. On that night David did the very thing he lamented about others: he trusted his kingship instead of the Lord who put him in his position. In the presence of those who brought him Bathsheba, he did not put his hope in the Lord's name. Instead, he sought refuge in his destructive behavior.

If only David had listened to his own counsel, to his own psalms, to his own beautiful confessions of God's greatness, then boredom would have been obliterated in his life. An un-bored David would not have pursued Bathsheba. He would have gazed on the beauty of the Lord, thought about the Lord through the watches of the night, and commanded his soul to trust in God.

If only we would listen to our own advice. If only kings, parents, teachers, and preachers would heed their own counsel.

Our Bored Lives

Blaise Pascal, the famous mathematician and theologian, wrote, "All of humanity's problems stem from man's inability to sit quietly in a room alone."[8] Pascal's statement is an accurate indictment on humanity, on our hearts. We are bored creatures, always looking for something to satisfy us. Just as David could not sit quietly in his room alone that fateful night, our hearts are restless too. While we often look for experiences and possessions to relieve our boredom, neither brings us true satisfaction.

Experiences Fail

Our society has advanced incredibly since David strolled the roof of the palace, yet many of us are still bored. We can travel the world, watch anything we desire on our smartphones, read more books than any people who have ever lived, and eat an array of dishes that did not exist years ago. For example, in the last decade both Instagram and the Luther Burger, a hamburger patty sandwiched between two donuts that serve as the buns, have entered our lives with great buzz and fanfare. What did we ever do without these inventions? Yet as you read this there is somebody, somewhere in a new restaurant eating a burger smashed between two donuts, sipping on the newest and hippest craft beer, occasionally glancing at a flat-screen television, while stalking friends and celebrities on Instagram on the latest iPhone. And still bored.

Anything we experience in this world may temporarily numb our boredom, but it will not eliminate it and it will not satisfy us. Essena O'Neill was an Internet celebrity who many teenage girls admired. With more than half a million Instagram followers, companies paid her to wear and post pictures of their products as she chronicled her thrilling and seemingly almost perfect life. She made headlines and shocked many people when she abruptly walked away from all her social media platforms. After her decision she wrote, "I can't tell you how free I feel without social media. Never again will I let a number define me. IT SUFFOCATED ME." While her posts seemed effortless to her fans, she labored and agonized over maintaining her public persona.[9] She experienced what many teenage girls long for and it did not satisfy; it only suffocated.

Possessions Fail

Our experiences will not ultimately remove our boredom, but neither will our possessions. They always fail us as the newness quickly fades. Stephanie Land is a gifted author who wrote a fascinating piece about her two years cleaning houses to support her daughters. Because the company she worked for encouraged her to slowly clean houses in order to maximize profit, she paid close attention to the details of the families in the large, expensive houses she was cleaning. She learned what couples slept in different bedrooms, which families were addicted to porn, and what medicine use moved from prescription to recreation. She vacuumed elementary kid's bedrooms that were bigger than her apartment, and saw families spend exuberant amounts of money, such as the receipt she found for a blanket that was more expensive than her car. After two years of cleaning large homes filled with empty lives, Stephanie concluded the larger the home, the harder the people worked to afford it, and the more pills were needed to get through the misery. She vowed to never have a house larger than she could clean herself.[10]

Our boredom does not begin with large social media followings or big houses. It begins with the sin that plagues us from birth, from the time our mothers conceived us. The reason we cannot sit still in a room is because of the sin in our hearts. We are bored because, in our sinful rebellion against the God who created us and loves us, we seek fulfillment and happiness in things other than Him, in things that fail to satisfy.

True Satisfaction

After scouring scientific research on boredom and interviewing hundreds of people about their own personal boredom, a group of psychologists concluded that boredom is much more than simply "not having anything to do," especially in our culture as there is always something to occupy time. Rather the psychologists concluded that boredom is "the unfulfilled desire for satisfying activity." In other words, people are bored because their desire to be satisfied is unfulfilled.[11]

We are perpetually bored and naturally restless unless we look to the One who never bores, to the only One who satisfies. Augustine wrote, "You have made us for yourself, O Lord, and our heart is restless until it rests in you."[12] If our hearts rest in Him, we can sit in room and rest. If our hearts do not rest in Him, we won't rest anywhere. C. S. Lewis wrote, "If I find in myself desires which nothing in this world can satisfy, the only logical explanation is that I was made for another world."[13]

Broken Cisterns

The Lord calls our restless wandering from Him a double evil as we simultaneously abandon Him *and* seek satisfaction in something else. Whatever else it may be, it is less than Him, and He calls it "a cracked cistern that cannot hold water" compared to Him, "the fountain of living water."[14] A cracked cistern is terrifying for people who depend on cisterns to drink, because it means they'll thirst to death. He is a fountain of living water that continually quenches, and seeking something else is as ludicrous as relying on a cracked cistern for water.

The heavens are "appalled and shocked" at our foolish trade as we exchange our Creator for creation, our Savior for things that can never fully save, and the only One who can satisfy our souls for things that are unable to do so.

Foolish trades are always appalling and shocking. For example, a father joyfully and carefully prepares the perfect steak on the grill for his middle school son, the filet mignon he personally picked out from the butcher shop and marinated in his special seasoning for the last twenty-four hours. He cooks it just right, and proudly delivers it simmering to the kitchen table as the aroma from the grill rushes inside and fills the kitchen. The son takes one bite, winces, and asks his mother if he can have a Pop-Tart for supper instead. The father is appalled at his son's choice and shocked that his gracious gift is traded for something so much less.

Or imagine if the Golden State Warriors decided to trade Steph Curry, one of the greatest pure shooters in basketball history. Fans would be livid. People would picket and protest. The decision to trade Curry would be the center of conversation on sports radio and television. But imagine if Curry was traded not for another professional basketball player, but for a middle school boy who had not yet hit his growth spurt. Fans would be utterly shocked because the trade would be beyond any reason.

Our decision to trade God for something else is infinitely more appalling. The distance in greatness between the steak and Pop-Tart, between a NBA super-star and the scrawny middle school sharp shooter, is infinitely less than the distance in greatness between the Lord and everything else. Nothing comes close to comparing to Him. He alone is God. The heavens are appalled and shocked because God is immensely greater than anything else we could behold.[15]

When our hearts are not filled with wonder for God, we wander from Him, which is why true boredom is a sin. If we are bored we are looking for something other than God because God never bores. Boredom is proof our hearts have wandered from Him and are not resting in the only One who can give us rest. Jared Wilson insightfully wrote:

> Boredom is a sin so long as Christ is infinitely beautiful.... Because the good news proclaims the unsearchable riches of Christ, who opens the window looking out on the eternal mystery of the Trinity, it is endlessly absorbing, dazzlingly multifaceted. When we are bored, it can only be because we have stopped looking at Jesus. He can't be boring. If we find him boring, it's because we are boring. The deficiency is ours, not his.[16]

Boredom is sin because we are telling God that we are not looking at Him because we do not believe Him, in that moment, to be ultimately worthy of our attention and affection. Our boredom says, "God is not enough for us so we are looking for something else." Though boredom may not lead to murder and adultery, it always indicates a dethroning of God and an enthroning of something other than Him.

David's implosion shows us that not only is boredom sin, but it also leads to other sins.

Boredom can lead to materialism. If you long for a new car, boat, or house because you are bored with your status in life, then you are looking to the car, boat, or house to bring something to you that only He can bring. And you are telling Him that He is not enough for you.

Boredom can lead our minds astray. If you are looking at pornography or Facebook stalking a crush from high school behind your spouse's back, you are not merely saying you find your spouse boring, you are declaring that God and His plan for your life is boring.

Boredom can lead to gossip and slander. If you need to be in the know, need to have your mind tickled with rumors about someone else because it makes you feel alive or important, you are insisting that God is not enough.

Boredom can lead to living for and from one vacation to the next, or one weekend to the next, and not faithfully stewarding your current responsibilities. Conversely, boredom can lead you to seek your identity in your craft, in your career. Either way, boredom means you are looking at something other than Him. In short, boredom is whoredom.

Boredom Is Whoredom

David is not the only one who has committed adultery. As we have pursued things other than God, we have cheated and been unfaithful. We must recognize the nature of our sin, the nature of turning away from the Lord who has given Himself for us. Boredom means we have forsaken our first love and chased other lovers.

In Scripture, God compares our wandering to an unfaithful spouse who insists on taking other lovers.[17] To grab His people's attention and call them back to Himself, God told one of Israel's prophets, Hosea, to marry an unfaithful woman named Gomer to give Israel a picture of their unfaithfulness. Hosea's wife left him for others, just as we leave our Lord for others. Yet Hosea pursued his own wife and purchased her from slavery just as the Lord pursued us and purchased us with His own blood.[18] Instead of having our hearts set on our first love, on the One who loved us first and wooed us to Himself in the midst of our sin, we pursue other gods.

The only way to be satisfied is to look to the Lord because only He is the fountain of living water. The quicker we realize and the more frequently we are reminded that He is the only One who will not bore, the better we are. Our boredom is a blessing if it causes us to leave behind what bores us for Him.

Blessed Boredom

I love watching my daughters on Christmas morning. Our routine is pretty standard; they run downstairs once we give the green light, usually well before their normal wake-up time of 7:00 a.m. After quickly emptying their stockings and mumbling a few half-hearted "thanks" for gummy worms and a new toothbrush, they rush to the Christmas tree to find an unwrapped present—one for each daughter. It is great fun to watch my girls go ballistic over something they have wanted for months: a Doc McStuffins kitchen, a bike, an electric scooter, or the Baby Alive that goes to the bathroom. After their initial excitement settles down, we pass out the other presents and take turns opening them. The girls spend most of Christmas day playing with their new toys, showing them to friends in the neighborhood, and deciding the place of prominence the toys will receive in their rooms.

When they go to bed on Christmas night, they do not grasp how quickly the toys will lose their luster. Within a few months, though, tassels on their handlebars have fallen off, stickers on their toys have faded, and the baby doll does not go to the bathroom on command. Within a few months, the toys have broken pieces, and the promise that these toys will satisfy is broken too.

I recently pointed out to my daughters that they have already moved on from toys they thought they would never tire of, toys only a few months before they longed to have: "I want you to recognize that things you want will never be enough for you. They will never satisfy you."

Eden, my oldest, responded, "But is that good Daddy? Is it good that these toys don't satisfy me, that I don't ride the scooter that much anymore?"

"Absolutely it is good! God is being so good to you to show you that these things are not what will make you happy. Only God can make you really happy."

I borrowed my response from Augustine, who my daughters have never heard of but who wrote to God, "You were being the more gracious the less you allowed anything to grow sweet to me that was not You."[19]

God is gracious and kind to keep us from being satisfied in anything other than Him. Because if we were, we would fail to see the misery of our boredom and we would fail to look to Him. Boredom is a blessing if it helps you see Him as the One who never bores and always quenches.

For my daughters, the toys make terrific gifts but terrible gods. I don't want my daughters to enjoy the toys less, but I want them to enjoy God more. And, of course, I need to listen to my own counsel.

Work, homes, relationships, hobbies, toys, and other things we can pursue are gifts from above, blessings from God. Enjoying them as gifts is vastly different from bowing to them as gods. When we bow to Him, we enjoy the blessings more not less. When we seek Him, the Giver of all good things, He gives greater joy than the blessings He provides can give.

Broken Vows from Broken Cisterns

We see the frustration of broken cisterns all around us. If you will look and listen you will see the thirst everywhere you look.

Boat owners joke about the two best days in a boat owner's life: the day the boat was bought and the day the boat was sold. If the boat delivered on the joy it promised, people would not celebrate the sale. But the headaches of boat ownership, from maintenance to unexpected costs, become more significant than the days enjoyed on the water.

When Tom Brady won his third Super Bowl, and seemingly had everything a famous athlete could desire, he confessed in a *60 Minutes* interview that he wonders, "Why do I have three Super Bowl rings and still feel like there is something greater out there for me? . . . I think, God, it's got to be more than this."[20]

On his track "No Love," Lil Wayne rapped that the rap game he has given himself to has broken her promise to him: "Married to the game but she broke her vows. That's why my bars are full of broken bottles and my nightstands are full of open Bibles." The industry has not delivered on her promise to him, so he confessed to searching for something else in bottles and Bibles.

The pithiest line in the movie *Miss Sloane* is at the end and captures well the pain of our attempts to alleviate our boredom through achievements and accomplishments. Sloane, the main character, is a talented, savvy, and effective lobbyist. She has found her worth and identity in her career, and though she seems to have it all together, there is immense emptiness beneath the surface. Her obsession with winning in her career costs her greatly and she finally comes to the conclusion that "Career suicide is better than suicide by career." Meaning, it is better to destroy your career than be destroyed by your career. Her career, which seemed anything but boring, was ultimately not enough.

While we join David in breaking our vows to the Lord, everything in this world that has promised freedom and happiness has broken vows to us. You have been deceived by everything that has promised you joy. Everything but Him. It is better to walk away from the broken cisterns that won't quench than to continue to offer yourself to them because all they will leave you with is a parched mouth.

Turn Your Eyes

On the roof, David turned His eyes away from the Lord and toward Bathsheba. Though she was a beautiful woman, her beauty did not compare to the Lord's beauty. When we read a Psalm that David wrote later in his life, we get the sense that he learned from this empty season of rebellion. While in the desert, fleeing from his son who staged a revolt against him, David wrote these words:

> God, you are my God; I eagerly seek you.
> I thirst for you;
> my body faints for you
> in a land that is dry, desolate, and without water.
> So I gaze on you in the sanctuary
> to see your strength and your glory.
> My lips will glorify you
> because your faithful love is better than life.
> So I will bless you as long as I live;
> at your name, I will lift up my hands.
> You satisfy me as with rich food;
> my mouth will praise you with joyful lips.
> When I think of you as I lie on my bed,
> I meditate on you during the night watches.
> (Ps. 63:1–6)

As David lay in his bed, he thought of the Lord through the watches of the night. He did not stroll around and look for something else. He was content to sit quietly in his room because he was satisfied as he gazed on the strength and glory of God.

If you are "just in a phase of life that is boring," you are in a phase of life where you are not staring at God. When you are not staring at Him, you will find something else to stare at. And as you stare at something else other than Him, your heart will be drawn from Him.

Don't ignore your boredom.

If you are bored by your career, stop looking at your career. If you are bored in your relationships, stop looking at your relationships. If you are bored with your possessions, stop looking at them. Instead:

> *Turn your eyes upon Jesus*
> *Look full in His wonderful face*
> *And the things of earth will grow strangely dim*
> *In the light of His glory and grace.*[21]

Isolation and boredom weakened the foundation of David's character, and they were fueled by *pride*.

Chapter Five

Believe
in Yourself

*Pride is spiritual cancer. It eats up the very possibility
of love, or contentment, or even common sense.*
— C. S. Lewis

Many kids imagine throwing the game-winning touch-down, hitting a last second shot, or saving a game with an interception for their favorite professional team. To actually play in the pros, though, is highly unlikely.

While kids, and often their parents, dream of making it to the pros or "playing on Sundays," few actually do. Take basket-ball for example. According to the National Collegiate Athletic Association (NCAA), 1 percent of high school basketball play-ers play collegiate basketball at a Division One school and 1 percent of college basketball players play in the NBA. To play in the NBA, you have to be in the top 1 percent of the top 1 percent. The odds are not in your favor.[1]

The more staggering statistic is not how few make it to the top of the game, but what happens after they get there. One would think that with all the preparation and work required to make it to the top, that those who play sports professionally would be well prepared to maximize the opportunity, to take advantage of their lucrative earnings to secure a future for themselves and their families. Sadly, the opposite is the norm.

From a statistical point of view, becoming an elite professional athlete means a high likelihood of a very bleak financial future. A shocking number of professional athletes struggle greatly or are completely broke within a few years of retirement. For example, of the players who leave the NFL, 78 percent are bankrupt within five years.[2] Guys who earned millions of dollars in a few years lose it all or have little left from their time at the summit of sports.

What happens?

Billy Corben directed *Broke*, which chronicled how athletes crumble into financial ruin. Corben pointed to pride, saying "The athletes have a tremendous pride and ego that is fueled by a fan base that reveres them as these indestructible heroes and icons. That feeds their hubris in business, when they are making investments and they think they are going to be successful in areas most people tend to fail."[3] Another writer called their struggle "ego bleed."[4] These athletes are so dominant in sports that they wrongly assume their dominance on the field will translate to the marketplace and boardroom. Their ego in one area of their life bleeds over to other areas and ignites their downfall.

Ego. Pride. Hubris. They always precede a downfall.

Not Just Athletes

L. J. Rittenhouse is known for her ability to predict the future performance of a company by studying the leader's quarterly shareholders letters to examine the candor of the leader scientifically. She knows the "corrosive impact of inflated egos," so she searches for words that reveal pride in a leader because "arrogant, self-serving, out-of-touch CEOs present a serious financial risk."[5]

Pride was at the center of David's disobedience and destruction. David's pride did not begin the night he sent for Bathsheba, but it was the night it bled over to his decision-making about how to spend an evening.

When David asked who the beautiful woman was, the woman who lived in the house he was able to see from his roof, the woman he wanted more than he wanted his own integrity, he discovered she was married. You get a sense, as you read the story, that the servant David sent to find out about the woman knew the treachery that was about to unfold as he sheepishly asked, "Isn't this the wife of Uriah?" David's response was to send a servant to get her anyway. After all, David was king and the king got whatever he wanted.

Earlier in his life, David humbly asked God to keep him in the shadow of His wings as he was grateful for the Lord's provision of a cave for his residence.[6] When David was weak before God, he was actually strong. But when he felt strong, he was very weak. He did not seek refuge in the arms of God but in the arms of a woman. When he abandoned his weakness before God and walked in pride, he walked toward his own demise.

Entitlement = Ingratitude

Perhaps David felt entitled to the palace and entitled to bring a married woman to his room because he had served the people of Israel extremely well, defeated their enemies, energized the capital city, and given a sense of national pride to the people. He felt he deserved whatever he wanted, deserved more than he currently had. David's sense of entitlement increased as his pride increased. He forgot that all his victories and all the blessings he enjoyed were only because God had graciously given them.

Entitlement always rises as pride rises. It is impossible to be filled with humility and a sense of entitlement at the same time. Whenever we feel we are owed something it is because we have forgotten that God is the One who gives all good things.

David's belief that he was entitled to Bathsheba revealed that, in this moment, he was not filled with gratitude for God and His blessings. God was the One who took David from watching sheep to leading all of Israel, from sleeping in fields and caves to sleeping in a palace, from being one whose family considered him an unlikely candidate for king to the king everyone respected and revered. Tragically, all of that was not enough for David on the night he gave the order for servants to bring Bathsheba to him. He was ungrateful for God's blessings, and instead of using the throne to serve others, he used the throne to serve himself.

When we walk in humility, we are grateful for what the Lord has provided. When we walk in pride, we are not satisfied and want more. Pride fuels ingratitude and entitlement. Humility destroys them both.

Gratitude occurs when our expectations are exceeded, when what we feel we are owed is surpassed by what we actually receive. For example, imagine that on your next night away from home, someone pays for and gives you a key to a room at a Holiday Inn Express. Are you grateful or disappointed? Well, your answer depends on what you expected your accommodations to be.

If you expected a room at a Ritz-Carlton, you are definitely disappointed. There isn't a sitting room, an extra little TV in the bathroom, and there isn't organic lotion imported from an island in the Pacific. No one places chocolates on your bed and pulls the covers back for you at the Holiday Inn Express. The television is not even hanging on the wall; it is one of those old school big TVs that, sigh, is not even high definition. How dare they! Your expectations are not met, and you are disappointed because you wanted more.

If, however, you expected a room at an old college dormitory with community showers and bathroom stalls without doors on them, you are blown away with gratitude. You have your own shower! And the water is warm and soothing instead of cold and violent! There are sheets on the bed! Because your expectations are surpassingly exceeded, you go to bed that night extremely grateful. You chuckle as you doze off with the realization that you have two pillows; oh, what grace has been bestowed!

When we remember we were slaves and prisoners to our own sin, we are deeply thankful for liberation because we know that we are only owed death because of our sin. Just as our freedom and forgiveness is a gift, so is every moment and every breath. Christians believe that we only have what we have received, and we have only received because God is gracious, kind, and generous to us. When we humbly start the day with that perspective, we are grateful for all He provides. When we live as if we are owed something, it is because pride resides deeper in our hearts than we realize.

The First and Great Sin

While the explosive sins of isolation and boredom were active in David's heart, pride was the first to take root. It was his pride that pulled him into isolation, his pride that shrugged off accountability, and his pride that drove him away from others and toward the absurd thinking that he did not need anyone. It was also pride that fostered boredom in David's heart. His pride caused him to see himself as greater than he was, which inevitably led him to view God's blessings as less than they were.[7] His pride caused him to look at himself more and God less, which amplified and multiplied his boredom and isolation.

We get the term *narcissism* from the Greek mythological figure Narcissus, who fell in love with his own image. He was a hunter and was well known for his beauty. His arch-nemesis was named, well, he was named Nemesis, and he lured Narcissus to a pool where Narcissus saw his own reflection. Narcissus was in awe of himself and stared at his reflection until he died. His pride paralyzed him and prohibited him from walking in wisdom. In some versions of the story, he killed himself because his own image could not quench and satisfy him. Like the mythical Narcissus, David was preoccupied with himself and it led to his own demise.

Narcissus' enemy knew the way to ruin him was to get him to be fascinated with himself. Your enemy is the same way. Your enemy, the devil, prowls around like a roaring lion looking for someone to devour, and if you are consumed with yourself instead of the Lord, you will self-destruct.[8]

Our enemy knows pride very well. It was pride that made the devil the devil, as he was consumed with his own beauty and desired to be equal with God in majesty and authority.[9] Pride was also the first sin of Adam and Eve. God instructed them to enjoy His creation and to simply not eat from one tree, the tree of knowledge of good and evil. The tree represented the authority to decide and declare what is good and evil. By eating from the tree, Adam and Eve insisted that *they* were in charge (not God), that *they* would decide what is right and good and best.[10] In their pride, they removed God as the ruler of their lives and put themselves in His place.

Pride is the first sin in our lives too, and it leads to a multitude of other sins. When we insist on deciding what is best for our lives instead of trusting His rule and reign, our rebellion will touch all areas of our lives.

Pride is the great sin because of its devastating impact. Because of Satan's pride, God kicked him out of heaven and relegated him to wreaking havoc on this world for a season until the moment of his final destruction. Adam and Eve's prideful rebellion was the sin that brought death, despair, and brokenness to the perfect world God created. Pride is the great sin in our lives too, the sin that hurts others and us and declares war with God, as He opposes the proud. C. S. Lewis wrote:

> Pride has been the chief cause of misery in every nation and every family since the world began. Other vices may sometimes bring people together: you may find good fellowship and jokes and friendliness among drunken people or unchaste people. But Pride always means enmity—it is enmity. And not only enmity between man and man, but enmity to God. . . . There is no fault that makes a man more unpopular, and no fault which we are more unconscious of in ourselves.[11]

Though pride is the first and great sin, we rarely recognize it in ourselves. We tend to notice specks of pride in others while planks of pride remain in our eyes, obscuring how we view everything. To mix metaphors—not only does pride distort how we see everything, but we also struggle to smell its stench in our lives.

Not Smelling Our Stench

When a team from Procter & Gamble developed Febreze, they were convinced they had a product that people would rush to purchase. Their confidence was based on their work researching and talking to people about the desire for a product that would eliminate bad odors, not just overwhelm bad odors with good ones. People the research team polled were grateful and excited about the launch of Febreze, but when the product launched in select markets, very few people bought it. The team was dumbfounded, and decided to visit people who said they loved Febreze to learn why they were not buying. In their follow-up interviews, the research team discovered that people were not purchasing because they believed there were no bad odors to eliminate in their lives.

One of the homes they visited belonged to a woman who had nine cats living with her. The researchers could smell the cats even before the front door was opened to welcome them inside. Once inside the home, the smell was so overwhelming that one of the researchers gagged. When the woman was asked about the cat smell, she replied, "It's usually not a problem. I notice a smell about once a month."[12] Armed with the insight that people often fail to smell their own surroundings, Procter & Gamble repositioned and successfully re-launched

Febreze as the way to finalize a cleaning process, not as a product solely for undesirable odors.

We are plagued with the same problem. We often do not smell the stench of our pride. While we quickly notice the stench on someone else, we are often oblivious to the pride in our own lives, noticing it "maybe once a month or so."

How can we recognize pride in our own lives so we can avoid implosion? How can we see the first and great sin at work in us? Let's learn from other kings.

Learning from Kings

David was not the only king of Israel to read and believe his own press, to behave as if he was entitled to more, to be ruined by pride. Pride ruined David's predecessor, Saul. Early in his role as king, Saul offered sacrifices to the Lord, though the Lord had made clear that these were only to be brought by priests. Saul acted as if those commands didn't apply to him and he could do anything he wanted as king.[13]

On another occasion, Saul disobeyed God's command to destroy everything that belonged to an enemy army, but Saul only killed the worthless and unwanted sheep and cattle. In his pride, he believed his ideas and insights were better than the Lord's instructions. Because he was victorious in battle, he felt emboldened to follow his own wishes.[14]

Though David watched pride destroy Saul, he failed to live in humility as his inner life deteriorated. Like David, we can observe pride in others while it simultaneously destroys us. You may be an expert in diagnosing pride at work, while not seeing it in your own heart. You may be quick to detect pride in your friends or in your spouse, while not realizing that it is actually your own pride that has you looking for it in others. The problem with pride is that you may have managed prideful employees, may have parented entitled kids, coached ego-driven players, and lamented their pride—while yours remained.

David was not the only king who failed to apply the lessons from previous kings. Years after David, Uzziah was another king for God's people, and his story of pride is terribly tragic. For years he walked with the Lord and feared Him, and the Lord gave him success. He built a massive army, equipped them with the latest gear and weapons, destroyed enemies, and brought great security to the people. He was well-known and well-loved in far away places. People likely named their kids after Uzziah, pretended to be him in childhood games, and told stories over dinner about times they met him or even saw him from a distance.

"But when he became strong, he grew arrogant, and it led to his own destruction."[15]

Just as Saul, years before, egotistically performed the duties of a priest, Uzziah entered the holy place in the temple that was reserved for the priests. When the priests confronted him on his sin, he responded with anger, and the Lord struck him with leprosy. Because of his leprosy he lived in isolation the rest of his life, and his lasting legacy to future generations was merely, "He had a skin disease." His reputation deteriorated from being known as a great and mighty leader to simply being known as the man with leprosy. In his pride, he destroyed himself.

The clear indications of pride in Uzziah's life can help us recognize pride in our lives, can alert us to what we often miss. We often cannot see or smell our own pride, but if there is *apathy* for the Lord, *disregard* for His commands, or *resentment* of accountability, then pride has taken a firm and growing hold of our hearts.

Apathy toward God

Earlier in his life, Uzziah was instructed in the fear of God, but as Uzziah grew in power and fame, he became more impressed with himself and less impressed with God. He had an inflated view of himself, believing he could go wherever he wanted, even into the place in the temple reserved for the priests.

If our awe for God decreases, our apathy toward Him increases. If we don't hold wonder for Jesus and what He has done for us, He is small in our lives and we are big. If our minds are not captivated by His greatness, drawn to thinking of Him, and filled with increasing gratitude for His mercy toward us, we are apathetic toward Him. The more we think of ourselves, the less we think of Him.

Disregard for His Commands

Earlier in his life, Uzziah "did what was right in the LORD's sight,"[16] but as pride filled his life, he began to disregard the Lord's instruction. He wanted to experience what the priests were able to experience, so he shrugged off the Lord's command.

Whenever we attempt to reason our way out of obeying the Lord, pride has consumed our minds and driven us to foolishness. The foolishness often expresses itself in really dumb things we say about the Lord. In our pride we can even use "let us pray about that," as an excuse to delay obeying what the Lord has already made clear.

A man hears a sermon about serving others, and tells his wife, "I am going to think and pray about that." A couple knows their neighbor is in need and continually say to one another, "Let's be praying about helping." A busy working mother receives a challenge to invest time reading Scripture and responds with, "Yeah, uh, sure, I will pray about reading my Bible."

There are many things we do not need to pray about: commands the Lord has already made absolutely clear. We need to pray for His grace and joy *as* we obey Him, but not to determine *if* we should obey Him. Our tendency to negotiate with His commands and to contemplate if they actually apply to us reveals that we often believe our way is better. In our pride, we think we know what is best for "our" lives, forgetting that our lives are not ours anymore. If we are His, our lives are His.

Resentment of Accountability

When Uzziah was successful, he received instruction from the teacher Zechariah. He once listened to godly people, but as he became prideful, he began to shun counsel. He stopped learning from others and acted as if no one could hold him accountable because no one knew what it was like to be him. Instead of responding to the priests' rebuke with humility and repentance, he resented their truthful confrontation and responded with anger and rage.

A clear sign of pride is the belief that we can help and teach others, but that we have moved beyond needing help and instruction. If we stop learning from others, pride has deceived us into thinking we are above instruction and counsel. The more we are filled with pride, the fewer people there are who we feel can offer encouragement and help to us.

Be Killing Pride

John Owen wrote, "Be killing sin or sin will be killing you."[17] Unless we are killing pride right now, it is killing us. If we approach pride passively, it will consume and corrupt us. If we don't decide to kill pride we are deciding to allow pride to take root and pull us further from God and closer to implosion.

The way to slay pride is not to focus on your pride. Or even on your humility. If you focus on either, you are focusing on yourself. The way we walk in humility is to look to Him, not ourselves. When our minds are focused on Him, our thoughts about Him grow bigger and our thoughts about ourselves grow smaller. C. S. Lewis wrote that a truly humble man "will not be thinking about humility: he will not be thinking about himself at all."[18] Therefore, humility is not demeaning yourself in attempts to prove yourself humble.

Insecurity is not humility. Insecurity is a focus on self and not a focus on Him. When we are insecure, we are in an earning posture, always attempting to qualify ourselves before God and others. Humility, however, rests in the approval freely given by God instead of feverishly and egotistically attempting to earn it. Overcoming insecurity and walking in humility requires continually looking to the One who has already approved us because of Christ. As we look to Him, we are both humbled and secured by His great love for us and gracious approval of us.

Pride is the antithesis of what it means to be a Christian. We are His because God humbled Himself for us, became a man, and put Himself on the cross in our place. His humiliation resulted in our salvation, and the salvation He has given produces a humble gratitude in us.[19]

Jesus reminded us that we became His when we humbled ourselves as children before Him (Matt. 18:3). Children trust their caregivers for everything, and we became His when we trusted Him for everything. Children throw themselves into the arms of those who love them, and we entered His kingdom when we threw ourselves into His grace. The Christian faith drives a stake into pride's heart, giving us absolutely nothing in ourselves to be prideful about. We are only His by His grace, not by anything we offer.

The way to enter His kingdom is through humility and increasing humility reveals that we are becoming more like Him. The closer we draw to Him the more we see our need for Him because the closer we draw to Him the more we grasp His holiness and our sinfulness. As an example, notice the progression of increasing humility in the apostle Paul's life.

For I am the **least of the apostles**, not worthy to be called an apostle, because I persecuted the church of God *(1 Cor. 15:9—written in AD 56)*.

This grace was given to me—the **least of all the saints**—to proclaim to the Gentiles the incalculable riches of Christ *(Eph. 3:8—written in early AD 60 or 61)*.

This saying is trustworthy and deserving of full acceptance: "Christ Jesus came into the world to save sinners"—and I am **the worst of them** *(1 Tim. 1:15—written between AD 62–64)*.

The more Paul matured in his faith the more sinful he saw himself. In a matter of years, he progressed from "I am the worst apostle in the group" to "I really am the worst Christian I know" to "I am the worst sinner on the planet." Some would read those verses and say Paul digressed. But Paul wasn't actually more sinful; he just saw himself more clearly in light of the Lord's holiness.

The more we look to God, the more we understand His holiness, thus realizing more fully how sinful we really are, which increases our gratitude for His grace. Because of Jesus, our joy does not diminish when we see ourselves as more sinful. Because of Jesus, our joy actually increases because we understand that His love and grace are even bigger and better than we first understood.

Humility increases as we step closer to the Lord, and it decreases as we step away from Him. As David's heart shifted from the Lord, his pride was on full display. Pride was the consistent theme in David's implosion. He did not attack pride, so pride attacked him.

We all struggle with pride, and God is gracious to confront us in our pride so we may repent quickly and not be consumed by it. Continuing in our pride is what will lead to our ruin. The way to avoid self-destruction is to recognize our pride and quickly repent, to own it and fall fast.

Fall Fast

When I lived in Cincinnati, I learned how to snow ski. Well, kind of. Those who love snow skiing would not call skiing in the Midwest actual skiing, but more like sliding down a hill on top of a sheet of ice. I am definitely not a great snow skier, not the guy who is boldly slashing through the most difficult double black diamond courses.

When skiing, or sliding down ice-packed hills, I fell often. Thankfully, I was never seriously hurt because if I felt I was losing control, I would tap out and fall. A friend taught me that. He told me to fall whenever I sensed I was losing control, not to fight it and ski more chaotically and more quickly, but just to own it and fall.

"Fall fast," he said.

The whole Christian life is to be one of falling fast—one of repentance.[20]

When you sense your heart wandering, fall fast.

If you fall fast you will hurt less, and you will hurt fewer people. Own your sin and repent before it spins recklessly out of control. On the slopes, those who fall fast don't hurt nearly as much as those who continue and build up more speed and ski recklessly out of control before falling. Out of control skiers not only hurt themselves, but they can also take out others with them. Those who fall fast limit their pain and the collateral damage that spreads to others.

When skiers fall fast, it is much easier to get up, much easier to continue without being hauled off the course in a stretcher and unable to ski for months. If you fall fast you can get up more easily.

During the events surrounding David's fall, he refused to fall fast. Instead he continued in a quick and relentless downward spiral. As he went to bed that tragic night he could have repented of his pride, his belief that he was owed whatever he wanted because of his accomplishments as king. He could have repented, confessed his weakness, and thanked God for all His blessings. But he kept going. He did not fall fast.

As he walked on the roof in boredom, David could have recognized his unholy restlessness. He could have remembered times in his life when God filled him with joy. He could have asked the Lord to restore joy to him but, in his pride, he kept looking to himself.

David kept strolling until he saw a beautiful woman bathing. As he looked, he could have turned away and confessed his lust and his pride, but he refused to fall fast.

When David learned from a servant that she was married, he could and should have stopped and fallen right there. He could have owned his sin, confessed his foolishness for even asking about her, gone back to his room and begged God to turn his heart back to Him. But David did not stop; he kept spinning out of control.

When Bathsheba walked into his palace, he could have stopped. He could have seen her as a beautiful bride who was committed to someone else, to a man who was fighting for him on a battlefield somewhere. But David continued in his sin.

After he slept with Bathsheba and learned she was pregnant, he could have stopped. He could have owned his sin, called her husband home, and sought forgiveness from the Lord and those he harmed. But David, in his prideful stubbornness, held tightly to his sin and the belief that he could fix all his own problems.

While we will continually struggle with pride, we can choose a better response. We can repent over and over again. When we allow pride to build and multiply, the implosion is much more painful and much more destructive. So repent quickly. Repent daily. Fall fast.

. . .

. . .

. . .

THE IMPLOSION	THE CONFRONTATION	THE CONFESSION	THE CELEBRATION
2 Samuel 11	2 Samuel 12	Psalm 51	Psalm 32

David did not fall fast, but he did repent when he was confronted. While in pride he ruined his life, in humility he started over again. The story does not end with David's implosion and ruin. Your story does not need to end in ruin either. Turn the pages to read of the confrontation and David's beautiful confession, his starting over.

2 Samuel 12:1–13

So the Lord sent Nathan to David. When he arrived, he said to him: There were two men in a certain city, one rich and the other poor. The rich man had very large flocks and herds, but the poor man had nothing except one small ewe lamb that he had bought. He raised her, and she grew up with him and with his children. From his meager food she would eat, from his cup she would drink, and in his arms she would sleep. She was like a daughter to him. Now a traveler came to the rich man, but the rich man could not bring himself to take one of his own sheep or cattle to prepare for the traveler who had come to him. Instead, he took the poor man's lamb and prepared it for his guest. David was infuriated with the man and said to Nathan: "As the Lord lives, the man who did this deserves to die! Because he has done this thing and shown no pity, he must pay four lambs for that lamb."

Nathan replied to David, "You are the man! This is what the Lord God of Israel says: 'I anointed you king over Israel, and I rescued you from Saul. I gave your master's house to you and your master's wives into your arms, and I gave you the house of Israel and Judah, and if that was not enough, I would have given you even more. Why then have you despised the Lord's command by doing what I consider evil? You struck down Uriah the

Hethite with the sword and took his wife as your own wife—you murdered him with the Ammonite's sword. Now therefore, the sword will never leave your house because you despised me and took the wife of Uriah the Hethite to be your own wife.' "This is what the Lord says, 'I am going to bring disaster on you from your own family: I will take your wives and give them to another before your very eyes, and he will sleep with them in broad daylight. You acted in secret, but I will do this before all Israel and in broad daylight.'" David responded to Nathan, "I have sinned against the Lord."

Then Nathan replied to David, "And the Lord has taken away your sin; you will not die."

THE
IMPLOSION
2 Samuel 11

THE
CONFRONTATION
2 Samuel 12

THE
CONFESSION
Psalm 51

THE
CELEBRATION
Psalm 32

Psalm 51

For the choir director. A psalm of David, when the prophet
Nathan came to him after he had gone to Bathsheba.

> Be gracious to me, God,
> according to your faithful love;
> according to your abundant compassion,
> blot out my rebellion.
> Completely wash away my guilt
> and cleanse me from my sin.
> For I am conscious of my rebellion,
> and my sin is always before me.
> Against you—you alone—I have sinned
> and done this evil in your sight.
> So you are right when you pass sentence;
> you are blameless when you judge.
> Indeed, I was guilty when I was born;
> I was sinful when my mother conceived me.

> Surely you desire integrity in the inner self,
> and you teach me wisdom deep within.
> Purify me with hyssop, and I will be clean;
> wash me, and I will be whiter than snow.

> Let me hear joy and gladness;
> let the bones you have crushed rejoice.

Turn your face away from my sins
and blot out all my guilt.

God, create a clean heart for me
and renew a steadfast spirit within me.
Do not banish me from your presence
or take your Holy Spirit from me.
Restore the joy of your salvation to me,
and sustain me by giving me a willing spirit.
Then I will teach the rebellious your ways,
and sinners will return to you.

Save me from the guilt of bloodshed, God—
God of my salvation—
and my tongue will sing of your righteousness.
Lord, open my lips,
and my mouth will declare your praise.
You do not want a sacrifice, or I would give it;
you are not pleased with a burnt offering.
The sacrifice pleasing to God is a broken spirit.
You will not despise a broken and humbled heart, God.

In your good pleasure, cause Zion to prosper;
build the walls of Jerusalem.
Then you will delight in righteous sacrifices,
whole burnt offerings;
then bulls will be offered on your altar.

Part 3

If You Want to Start Over . . .

Chapter Six

Confess

There is more mercy in Christ than sin in us.
— *Richard Sibbes*

When you are dealing with the fallout of an implosion, when you feel like you have absolutely ruined your life, when you are embarrassed by your sin and not wanting to see anyone at all, God is eager to forgive. When you are numb with the pain of your own absurd choices, the Lord pursues you. When you feel life is hopeless, the God of all hope wants you.

No matter how great your sin is, His grace is greater. Wondering if there is enough forgiveness for your sin is like a child wondering if there is enough water in the ocean to fill his sippy cup. No matter how much you feel you have ruined your life, you have not out-sinned God's grace.

If you will come to Him, He will receive you. If you will glance toward Him, He will run to you just as the father, in a story Jesus told, ran to his wayward son and kissed and clothed him before throwing a party.[1] More than you want to be for-given, He wants to forgive. More than you want to come home to Him, He wants you home. If you can't walk, crawl. He will receive you and shower you with His mercy and love.

But you must confess, and you must understand what you are confessing. That is the first step in starting over. You must come to Him humbly. David, when confronted, confessed his sin, and we have much to learn from his confession.

I am the world's worst journaler. Not the worst journaler among preachers or the worst journaler among all Christians, but the worst journaler the world has ever seen, the worst jour-naler to crack open a new Moleskine with clear eyes and a full heart committed to making this time different. I have bought journals and received them as gifts, tried soft covered and hard covered journals, started writing in journals with large writ-ing pads and smaller ones too. But the end result is always the same. Within a few entries my journal turns into a task list.

Thankfully David was a much better journaler than I. The Psalms give us a glimpse into his personal prayer journal. Because of the psalms David wrote, we don't have to guess what David was thinking or praying at important moments in his life. And Psalm 51 gives us unfiltered access into his response to God after he was confronted on his sin. The Psalm is beau-tiful, raw, honest, and desperate. It is loaded with truth about ourselves, about God, and about how we should approach Him—not only after an implosion but all of the time.

David penned Psalm 51 after the prophet Nathan confronted him, reminded him of how good God was to him, pointed out his rebellion, and pronounced the discipline the Lord would bring upon David. David's response to the confrontation was simple: "I have sinned against the LORD."[2]

Nathan assured David that, though there would be consequences for his sin, his sin was taken away. He was forgiven. As great as David's sin was, God grace and forgiveness was greater.

David's response was proof that he belonged to God. Though David's wandering from the Lord was a failure to live his identity as a man after God's heart, his confession revealed he knew and appreciated God's holiness and grace. David did not protest, make excuses, or argue with Nathan. He owned his sin and accepted the consequences.

David responded very differently than his predecessor, Saul. When Samuel, a prophet before Nathan, rebuked Saul for his disobedience to God, Saul responded with excuses. God had instructed Saul to completely destroy the Amalekites, a people who continually stood against God's people.[3] Saul partially obeyed, which is really to disobey. He kept the best cattle for himself instead of destroying everything. When Samuel confronted him, Saul did a lot of talking and offered reasons for his disobedience.

Excuse-making responses are very different than sin-confessing ones.

How we respond when confronted on our sin reveals who we really are. Only when we stop making excuses and start confessing our sin are we really ready to start over after an implosion. Responses filled with excuses, protests, and pointing out the faults of others only proves that one is not ready to receive and enjoy His forgiveness and start over.

Don't Follow Your Heart

In David's confession, he did not pray about his struggle with lust or issues with anger or control. He did not ask God for help with sexual purity, which one could expect since his downfall seemingly began with an adulterous affair. David, though, knew that the fundamental problem was deeper. Sexual restraint and anger management were not the main issues.

David's heart was the issue.

Jesus taught, "from the heart come evil thoughts, murders, adulteries, sexual immoralities, thefts, false testimonies, slander."[4] So, the root of David's lust was his heart. His adultery, murder, and lying all came from his heart. When the Bible speaks of our heart, it is speaking of the core of who we are, the center of our being. Even the "man after God's own heart" struggled with the depth of sin in his heart.

Because our hearts are wicked, deceitful, and beyond our own understanding, the advice to "follow your heart" is extremely cruel. Unless our hearts are fully devoted to the Lord, encouragement to follow our hearts is horrible counsel. Foolish and harmful decisions are made every single day because of that advice. Families have been ripped apart because moms and dads followed that advice. Careers have been derailed, relationships have been destroyed, and much has been lost as people follow their hearts to their own demise. David followed his heart to his own ruin, which is why his prayer of confession addressed the sin in his heart.

In his best-selling book, *How Not to Die*, Dr. Michael Greger describes the most common health-related ways people die, most common being heart disease.[5] Each year four hundred thousand people die in the United States because of their hearts. Hundreds of thousands of people ignore their diet, exercise, and the concerns expressed by their doctors. Because of the shocking data, the health care industry rightly and continually encourages people to care for their hearts. Not doing so leads to death.

Our spiritual hearts are even more important. To live without our hearts devoted to the Lord is to waste our lives and miss the joy He provides, and to die without Christ transforming the heart is infinitely worse than heart failure in this life.

The first few verses of Psalm 51 provide us great clarity about the depth of the problem with our spiritual hearts, and we get a devastating view of just how unhealthy our hearts are.[6] The Old Testament was written in Hebrew, and in these three verses David used three different Hebrew words to describe the comprehensiveness of our sin:

> Be gracious to me, God, according to your faithful love; according to your abundant compassion, blot out my rebellion (*pesha*). Completely wash away my guilt (*avah*) and cleanse me from my sin (*chatha*). For I am conscious of my rebellion, and my sin is always before me. (Ps. 51:1–3)

David's confession was not casual or flippant, and the three different words show just how serious he understood his wandering from the Lord to be. David owned his sin and confessed that his heart rebelled, shifted, and missed the mark of God's holiness.[7]

A Heart that Rebels

David asked the Lord to blot out his "rebellion," which is translated from the Hebrew word *pasha*. Our hearts are filled with willful rebellion against the One we owe our allegiance.

Nathan reminded David that the Lord had pulled him from the pasture, given him the palace, and provided everything David enjoyed. And in return, "David despised the Lord's command." David purposefully stayed home from war when his duty as king was to be with his men. David knowingly sent for Bathsheba when a servant cautioned him about her marital status.

What does "rebellion" look like? Imagine a father on the all-important eve of trash day. He enters his teenage son's room with a reminder of the responsibility to take out the trash. The son nods, but goes to bed without taking out the trash. Perhaps his disobedience is casual, unintentional, or stems from laziness. Maybe the kid deserves a pass? So, imagine the same scenario, ending in a different way. The father enters, issues the same reminder, but instead the son tells his father "no," and slams the door in his face. The son owes his good father allegiance, the father who has protected and provided for his son, but the son offers willful rebellion instead.

Our rebellion is not against man, but against God, against the eternal King of kings, the One to whom we owe all allegiance because of who He is and what He has done. Our rebellion is not accidental, but purposeful. Rebellion is not just a mistake. It is much more than accidentally leaving your cell phone charger in your hotel room, losing your keys, or forgetting to return a phone call. We know the difference between right and wrong, good and evil, and we chose evil. When we say "no" to God, we slam the door in His face.

A Heart that Shifts

David pleaded with the Lord to wash away his "guilt," which is translated from the Hebrew word *avah* and carries the connotation of being twisted out of shape. David's heart was not centered on the Lord; it was twisted and off course.

On the rooftop that dreaded night, David's heart was twisted out of shape. He was not satisfied in God so he was looking for something else to satisfy him. If he longed for comfort because he was alone, he did not find his comfort in God because his heart was twisted. If he was overwhelmed with the burdens of being king and viewed the affair as an escape, it was because his heart was twisted and he did not give his burdens to the Lord.

What does a shifting heart look like? The father asks his son to take out the trash on the eve of trash day. The son immediately jumps off the couch, empties every trash can, refills them with plastic bags, and carefully positions the trash at the road. It seems perfect, but on this night the son takes out the trash for himself and not for his dad. He is motivated by the hope that his dad will let him stay up late to continue playing video games and not by his love for his father. While parents may be tempted to be content with *avah*, as at least the trash gets emptied, the Lord longs for our obedience because we love Him, not because we want something from Him.

The twisting of our hearts means we can do the right things for the wrong reasons.

A doctor prays with a patient before surgery, and some people applaud. Possibly the doctor does so because he loves the Lord and wants to serve people. Or possibly he does so because he knows he will be affirmed. It depends and because our hearts shift, we cannot know with absolute certainty simply by looking at the actions.

A dad, whose kids have graduated, coaches little league and he appears to be investing in the next generation for all the right reasons. Maybe. Or maybe he is empty inside and needs to be needed. Maybe he coaches for himself. Because our hearts shift, we will never know the motivations beneath the surface.

A mother works hard for hours with her high school son on his homework. It seems, based on her Facebook posts, that she does so out of love for her son. Perhaps. Or perhaps her heart is twisted out of shape and she helps for herself as she finds her worth in how he performs at school. Not only is she miserable, but she also has saddled her son with expectations he cannot deliver on because only the Lord can withstand the weight of providing her significance and meaning.

Because our hearts are twisted out of shape, even our good deeds can be performed with sinful motivations. Because our hearts are sinful, even our good deeds are filthy before Him.[8]

A Heart that Misses the Mark

David asked the Lord to cleanse him from his *chatha*, which is translated "sin," and paints the picture of missing the mark or target. God is pure and perfect and none of us are, no matter how hard we try, how religious we are, or how often our parents told us we are awesome, amazing, and rock stars in everything we attempt. We have missed the mark and fallen woefully short of His holiness.

When David rejected community, he fell short of God's design for relationships. When David lusted after Bathsheba, he missed the mark of God's holy love. When David was bored, he missed the mark by failing to reflect on God's beauty. When he plotted Uriah's murder, he missed the mark of trusting God as the giver and taker of life. When he attempted the elaborate cover up, he fell short of God's truthfulness. Through every stage in his fall, David missed the mark.

Let's go back to the father on the eve of trash day to help us understand *chatha*. After the father asks his son to take out the trash, the son huffs and puffs as he jumps off the couch. He scurries through the house, does not empty the bathroom trashcans, drags the kitchen trash bag on the floor leaving crumbs in his wake, does not bother putting a new trash bag in the kitchen trash can, and rushes the trash to the street. He gives his father a "Are you happy now?" look as he sinks back into the couch. While he may call his attempt obedience, it falls well short of his father's reasonable standard.

Our lives are marked by missing the mark. Even on our best days, we fall short. We cannot hit the mark in our own goodness or effort. We are like a two-year-old who cannot throw a football to an open player in the end zone. No matter how much a parent or coach implores the toddler to try harder, the child is unable to hit the mark. We are like an archer who attempts to shoot an arrow from New York City to Miami. No matter how much the archer practices or what technique the archer employs, the mark will be missed. Encouragement to "give your best" will only frustrate the archer with the reminder that all of his best attempts are futile.

Because of our limited understanding of His holiness, we miss the mark more than we realize. Much more than the two-year old quarterback or the hopeless archer misses their marks. And encouragements to give our best don't help at all. We cannot help ourselves; we need to be helped. We cannot cure ourselves; we need God to cure us.

One Cure

My father and I struggle with high cholesterol, which is a major predictor for heart disease. After taking my wife, Kaye, to Maine the fall of our twentieth anniversary to enjoy the color of the autumn leaves, and eat a dozen Lobster rolls in five days, my cholesterol shot up to 280. Friends, family, and doctors all agreed I had to do something. Something had to change. The counsel, however, as to *what* to do varied greatly. The messages from a variety of voices are confusing: "Get on medication." "Don't even think about meds if you care about your liver." "Eat cinnamon." "Drink red wine." "Run." "Don't run, but lift weights." "Eat salmon a lot." "Only eat plants." So while there is agreement that cholesterol creates a problem for my heart, there is great disagreement on how to attack the problem.

Good news: there is absolute clarity about how to deal with the problem with our spiritual heart. There are not multiple ways to fix the problem, not multiple paths we can take. God's grace, given to us in Christ, is the only solution. Only Jesus is able to create a new heart in us and continually cleanse us.

Our hearts are not pure in need of good works and protection; they are wicked in need of grace and transformation. Because of our rebellion, guilt, and sin, we are unable to heal ourselves, but in need of the Lord to heal us.

David's confession is both agonizing and beautiful to read—agonizing because it confronts us with the wickedness in our hearts and beautiful because it points us to God's grace and forgiveness.

David confessed his sin fully and freely because he believed he would receive God's grace fully and freely. Not because he was worthy, but because God is good and gracious. Because God's mercy is greater than our sin, David prayed these phrases:

Wash away my guilt.
Cleanse me from my sin.
Purify me and I will be clean.
Wash me, and I will be whiter than snow.
Blot out all my guilt.
God, create a clean heart for me.

There is only one kind of human heart that is clean—one that is brand new.

A New Heart

If you are not yet a follower of Christ, you don't need to turn over a new leaf; you need a new heart. You don't need to change your behavior, make bolder commitments to try harder, or tweak a few things about your life. You need Jesus to give you a completely new heart. And that is exactly what

Jesus came to this earth to do. He came on a rescue mission to seek and save that which was lost, to rescue people from their sins. Jesus said "It is not those who are well who need a doctor, but those who are sick. I didn't come to call the righteous, but sinners."[9]

We are all sinners in need of Jesus, but not all recognize the reality. This is why an implosion can be the best thing to happen to someone. The moment that God uses to awaken us to our sinfulness and the offer of His grace. God is gracious to show us that we are sick and in need of Him. As painful as living in the fallout zone of an implosion is, God uses those devastating moments to invite us to die to our old lives and receive His mercy. If you are reading this filled with the sting of ruining your life, your ruin may be the best thing that could have happened to you. The Lord desires to use the ruin to bring you to Himself, to give you a new life and a new heart.

Jesus told people if they wanted to follow Him, "let him deny himself, take up his cross, and follow me."[10] Those who heard Jesus knew that He was speaking about death, as the cross was a vivid and brutal picture of brutality, suffering, and death. The way to become a Christian is not to try, but to die. Die to your righteousness and receive His. Die to defending your throne to bow to His. Die to treasuring less so you may treasure Him. Die to living your life to embrace His.

The Scripture teaches us that when a person becomes a follower of Christ, the person is a new creation, the old goes away, and the new comes.[11] Jesus told a religious man, a very good man named Nicodemus, that he must be born again. We cannot, of course, go back into the womb of our mother and start all over. Jesus meant that when we trust Him with our lives, He makes us completely new. So that we could be born again, Jesus was lifted up on the cross to take away sins and give forgiveness to those who would believe in Him.[12]

We are attracted to stories of new beginnings and fresh starts. There is a longing within us, given to us by God, for the story of ruined lives transformed by grace.

Jean Valjean is the main character in Victor Hugo's famous novel turned Broadway play turned Russell Crowe singing movie, *Les Misérables*. After spending nineteen years in prison for stealing bread, Valjean, prisoner number 24601, is released. He is ordered to carry a yellow passport, which marks him as an untrustworthy criminal and signifies his past to all he interacts with. Because of the yellow passport, Valjean is unable to find work or a place to stay. Until he knocks on the door of the bishop.

The bishop welcomes Jean Valjean into his home, treats him with respect and kindness, and provides a warm meal served with silver spoons. Valjean attempts to go to sleep in the comfortable bed given to him by the bishop, but he cannot stop thinking about the silver spoons. He wrestles with stealing them because he knows he could sell them for more than he made in nineteen years of prison labor, but the bishop has been so kind and generous. Valjean finally gives into the temptation, steals the silverware, and rushes off in the middle of the night.

The next day, as the bishop eats breakfast with backup spoons and absorbs complaints against Valjean from his assistant, there is a knock at their door. Several French police officers are there with Valjean, and Valjean knows that he will be sent back to prison for many years so he stands miserably before the bishop. The bishop greets Valjean and says, "You forgot the silver candlesticks that go with the silverware." The officers inquire if this is true, that Valjean was given the spoons, and the bishop assures them that it is true and asks if Valjean can be released. Speechless, Valjean has no idea how to respond. The bishop pulls him aside and says to him:

> Jean Valjean, my brother, you no longer belong to evil, but to good. It is your soul that I buy from you; I withdraw it from black thoughts and the spirit of perdition, and I give it to God.[13]

Valjean is never the same afterwards. The grace offered to him melts his heart and changes him forever. He becomes an extremely generous man, giving to the poor, caring for the sick, and assuming responsibility for an orphan girl.

Les Misérables is a beautiful story, and it points to the greater story, the good news we find in Christ. Christ came into our broken world to buy our soul, withdraw it from the darkness, and give it to God. Jean Valjean was purchased with silver candlesticks, but Christ purchased us from our empty way of life with His blood spilled for us on the cross.[14]

Jean Valjean loved greatly and gave generously because he was forgiven much. Jesus said that those who are forgiven much love much.[15] All of us who belong to Him have been forgiven much, but those whose lives have been ruined and then tasted the sweet grace and forgiveness of Christ are often the ones with the most vivid memory of His forgiveness.

Continually Cleansed

After becoming a Christian, we still struggle with sin. While we want to obey Him and please Him, we still live in a broken and fallen flesh surrounded by a broken and fallen world. David's story reminds us that godly people who have been changed by His grace can wander from the Lord. There is still plenty of confessing to do after we become a Christian, not only because we still struggle with sin, but also because we see our sin more clearly as we understand His holiness more fully.

When Nathan confronted David, Nathan assured him that his sin was already taken away. David was already forgiven because he belonged to God, yet David still confessed his sin. He desired his relationship with the Lord to be restored. He longed for God to bring joy back to him, the joy that his sin had stolen.

When we receive His grace and become a Christian, our past, present, and future sins are removed from us. All our sin is completely taken away, yet the Lord commands us to confess our sin continually so we may be reminded of His continual grace. While confession is good for the soul, Jesus is more so. As we confess our sins to Him, we are reminded of His forgiveness and our hearts are kept tender before Him. John, one of Jesus' disciples, wrote:

> If we confess our sins, he is faithful and righteous to forgive us our sins and to cleanse us from all unrighteousness. If we say, "We have not sinned," we make him a liar, and his word is not in us. My little children, I am writing you these things so that you may not sin. But if anyone does sin, we have an advocate with the Father—Jesus Christ the righteous one. He himself is the atoning sacrifice for our sins, and not only for ours, but also for those of the whole world. (1 John 1:9–2:2)

Jesus Is Our Advocate

We all want an advocate, someone who speaks for us, someone who represents us. If you desire to climb the ladder in a corporation, you are encouraged to have an advocate, someone who vouches for your leadership. When I have received speeding tickets, I have asked police officer friends to be my advocate and work to have the violation removed from my record. At times they extended mercy and at times they merely smirked in response, perhaps desiring to teach me justice (sigh).

Jesus speaks for you when you sin. He is constantly interceding for those who belong to Him, reminding the Father that the sin has already been taken away. Jesus is not advocating to an unwilling and unforgiving Father, but to the One who sent Him into the world to rescue us. As we confess our sins to Him, we are continually cleansed from all unrighteousness. He is faithful to forgive just as He has assured us He would.

Jesus Is Our Atonement

Because God is infinitely holy and sin is infinitely sinful, it cannot be swept under the rug or ignored. If sin is not punished, then God is not holy. As Jesus speaks for His own, He reminds the Father that the punishment for the sin has already been given. Christ has received the punishment in our place.

Whenever something goes visibly wrong in our culture, even things that are ultimately inconsequential, people immediately look for someone to blame, for someone to pay. When the wrong winner for Best Picture at the 2017 Oscars was announced, and movie stars were dumbfounded by the blunder, people quickly looked for the person responsible for the travesty.[16] People wanted someone to blame, from the announcers, to the person who handed them the envelope, to the guardian of the envelope, to those who planned the event. And while opinions varied about who should bear the responsibility, someone needed to absorb the wrath!

Humanity has always had a sense that we fall short and someone must pay for our sins. During the mythical Trojan War, the goddess Artemis punished Agamemnon, the Greek general, for evil deeds his soldiers committed. On their way to the war, Artemis caused the winds to stir, and the Greek ships were knocked violently into one another. To appease the wrath of Artemis, Agamemnon sacrificed his daughter to her, and Artemis' wrath was transferred from the winds and the waves to Agamemnon's daughter. With the anger of the goddess satisfied, the ships reached Troy without any more difficulty.

The Trojan War legend was written about one thousand years before Christ was born, and it shows that people throughout history, even those who believed in multiple gods, believed their sins must be dealt with, that the wrath of the gods must be satisfied.

Unlike the gods depicted in Greek mythology, our God does not demand that we make things right and bring a sacrifice. We are unable to make things right. Instead, He offered

His Son as the sacrifice for our sin. He did not demand a sacrifice, but gave one. All the punishment that we deserved was given to Jesus, and all the blessings and rewards that Jesus deserved are given to us.[17] Because He is our atonement, we can approach Him with confidence knowing that the sin we carried has already been carried to the cross.

Chapter Seven

Surrender

When Satan tells me that I am sinner, he comforts me immeasurably because Christ died for sinners.
— *Martin Luther*

I hate roller coasters. Actually I hate most rides, but I really hate roller coasters. It may sound ridiculous to you thrill-seekers, but my heart rate speeds up, my palms get sweaty, and anxiousness steals my appetite. When Kaye and I were first married, we went to a state fair (one of those fairs where eighteen-year-old chain-smoking guys with mullets and heavy metal T-shirts run the rides while texting on their flip phones). I threw up in the bushes, the funnel cake I ate, after riding the swings. Yes, I just admitted in writing that I got sick on the swings. You can imagine what roller coasters do to my psyche and my stomach.

Yet, I have ridden every single roller coaster at Disney World. Why would I put myself through such pain? Simple: my oldest daughter loves them. So I took her out of school, took her to Orlando for a few days, and hopped from park to park to ride every roller coaster with her. With sweaty palms, I waited in long lines, smiled and acted like nothing was wrong, and willingly put myself on every ride—even ones that go backwards and ones that go upside down. I bore and absorbed something I hated to be with my daughter who I love so much.

God hates sin. Because He is infinitely righteous and holy, sin is a deep violation of His character. Yet He loves us. He created us, knows everything about us, and wants us. He loves us in the midst of our sin, in the midst of our wandering and rebelling. In His grace, He endured the cross and absorbed what He hates—our sin and shame—so we could be forgiven and our ruin restored.[1] And God hates sin far more than I hate roller coasters.

Therefore, there is now no condemnation for those of us who are in Christ. Our sin was condemned in Jesus instead of being condemned in us. David's sin, his implosion, was placed on Jesus—though Jesus entered our world centuries after David's sin. God was eager and willing to forgive David because He knew that David's sin and punishment would be placed on Jesus.[2]

Uriah was unknowingly and unwillingly sacrificed to cover David's sin, a covering that was incomplete and insufficient. Jesus knowingly and willingly sacrificed Himself to cover

David's sin completely and fully. David sacrificed Uriah for himself and Jesus sacrificed Himself for David. And for you too.

David received discipline for his sin, but Christ received the punishment.[3] And Christ has already received all the punishment for your sin too, if you have surrendered to Him.

Not Everyone Surrenders

After being confronted, David did not take his sin lightly, and he did not view God's forgiveness as a small matter. His prayer is evidence that David hit the bottom, was broken, and was ready to enjoy and live in the grace of God.

Not all people find God's grace in the midst of their implosion. Years later some will look back on their ruin and be filled with gratitude for the wake-up call, for the discipline the Lord brought into their lives. Some, though, will push through the implosion, and continue in self-reliance and self-consumption. Instead of surrendering to Him and receiving mercy from Him, they remain unbroken in the midst of all the brokenness around them, unmoved despite everything around them being moved by their reckless actions. Friends and family who watched the ruin unfold, pray and wait and hope for brokenness, surrender, and a fresh start. When they don't yet see brokenness, they make comments like:

"He hasn't hit rock bottom yet."

"She is sorry, but only sorry for being caught."

"He is still defending himself."

"She is acting like everything is normal, like nothing happened."

Watching a friend refuse to turn from the sin that led to the implosion is often more difficult than watching the implosion. While the ruin was agonizing to watch, the lack of repentance can be even more frustrating. Some waste their implosion while others seize it as a catalyst to begin again, to turn from sin and turn to Christ.

In David's psalm of confession we see a picture of unconditional surrender to the Lord, what it looks like when we truly turn from sin and turn to Him. We can look to David's prayer as a litmus test for our own surrender. We can see if we are really ready to begin again.

What does surrender look like?

You Don't Blame Others

In David's prayer of confession and surrender, noticeably missing is the mention of anyone else. He did not attempt to assign even partial blame to another person, did not ponder aloud if God was going to hold someone else accountable. No, David took full responsibility.

He didn't blame Bathsheba. He did not pray, "God, I only wish she had not been on the roof that night," in a passive-aggressive way that we are often so gifted at deploying to shift some of the guilt from ourselves to others. He did not pray, "God, I want to offer some context" and mention how beautiful she was and how weak he was in comparison. He didn't set her up as an accomplice in the sin that took place in his palace.

He didn't blame the servants who brought Bathsheba to him and suggest that they were somehow involved. He did not even slightly throw them under the bus with statements like, "I only wish I had better people around me."

He didn't blame his context and complain about how no one fully understood him or all the pressure he faced as king. He did not blame his sin on a stage of life or his position or the struggles in his job. Instead, he owned his sin with phrases like "my sin is always before me" and "against You and You alone I have sinned."[4]

Sincere confessions contain no qualifiers. When the prophet Samuel confronted Saul on his disobedience to God, Saul blamed the people around him. He confessed his sin but with a qualifier, "Because I was afraid of the people, I obeyed them."[5] In other words, "I am guilty but I don't share in the guilt alone. These people influenced and tempted me." David confessed and surrendered, while Saul hedged on his confession by involving others.

Like apologies, any confession with a qualifier isn't really a confession.

The husband who has broken marriage vows and apologizes while pointing out the difficult season at work has not yet owned the full weight of the sin, but still seeks to share some of the weight with others. The employee who slandered others at the office and, when confronted, blames the office politics has not yet fully owned the sin.

To surrender yourself and your sin, you have to first own your sin. And if you look to blame others, you have not yet owned what needs to be surrendered.

When people play the blame game, they delay starting over, and waste time pointing fingers in attempts to absolve themselves. The more they explain, the more they make excuses, the more they reveal they are still fighting with God instead of humbly surrendering to Him.

You Don't Bargain with God

David made no attempts in his confession to bargain with God. He did not attempt to offer sacrifices, promise to obey God in other areas of his life, or ask what he could do to make it up to God. Instead he simply prayed, "You do not want a sacrifice or I would bring it, You are not pleased with a burnt offering."

As king, David knew the sacrificial system of Israel very well. David knew that God did not need a bull or a goat, as if God was hungry or in need. The sacrifices were designed by God to be a reminder to the people of their sin and to foreshadow the ultimate Sacrifice, Christ. David also knew that the Lord was frustrated with empty sacrifices, with people who went through the motions of bringing sacrifices with hearts that were far from the Lord. More than sacrifices, the Lord wanted the hearts of His people. He wanted David's heart, and that is what David offered.

Saul, as you would expect, responded in the exact opposite way when he was confronted. He planned to offer sacrifices to God as a means of bargaining. Samuel, the prophet who confronted him, responded by saying, "To obey is better than to sacrifice. To pay attention is better than the fat of rams."[6] God did not desire Saul's sacrifice, but demanded Saul's obedience. Saul was willing to give God a sacrifice but unwilling to follow with an obedient heart, and the Lord never took pleasure in those type of sacrifices.

We are a bargaining people. Often when workaholic parents neglect their kids, they subtly bargain with them by offering gifts instead of time. When a friend can't help you move into your apartment because she is "busy with some stuff," even though you helped the last 5 times she moved, she may offer to "make it up to you" in some other way. Or perhaps you have seen the boss who loses his temper and yells at a team member, and instead of taking responsibility and seeking forgiveness, he showers the person with compliments over the next few weeks, as if the kind words can wash away the mistreatment.

Psychologists have termed this phenomenon "moral licensing" to describe how people give themselves permission to act immorally after proving to themselves that they are good. In other words, people may act in virtuous ways after behaving in ways that cause them to feel immoral. Or people may give themselves license for immoral behavior after they feel they have earned the right with plenty of good behavior.[7] Moral licensing is bargaining with your own conscience.

Bargaining with God looks similar. People can give money, go on mission trips, and volunteer to serve at church in attempts to earn God's favor and make things up to Him. While giving, going, and serving are important, they must never be used as bargaining chips with God. Instead they must be appropriate responses of a surrendered heart to His grace and forgiveness, not attempts to make things right with Him.

We can't make things up to Him. Your sacrifice cannot make you right with God. Only Jesus' sacrifice on the cross makes you right with God. If you are still bargaining, you have not surrendered.

You Don't Believe in Yourself

When we read David's confession, we do not find any bold statements that he was never going to sin again. He did not declare that he was drawing a line in the sand and would never fall in such a way again. He did not promise to never look at a woman lustfully or struggle with temptation. There is not a hint of self-belief in his confession. He knew better. He had just destroyed his life and knew very well his inability to stand in his own strength.

Instead David prayed, "Restore the joy of your salvation to me"[8] because David needed the joy that comes from the Lord's rescue to motivate him. He asked the Lord to "sustain me by giving me a willing spirit"[9] because he knew he was unable to sustain himself and needed the Lord to hold him up and give him the willingness to obey. The reason David could not believe in himself is because, as he prayed, he was "guilty when he was born; sinful when his mother conceived him."

All of us are sinful from birth, so we are unwise to believe in ourselves. This, of course, does not make for a great greeting card to give to new parents. You won't find a card at Hallmark that says, "Congratulations on your new 8.8 ounce ball of sin!" The pastor at your church likely won't lead the congregation to "pray for the new sin babies" at the next child dedication service. Though I don't recommend we put that on celebration cards or lead child dedication that way, it is true. The cuteness of our baby pictures (well, some of our baby pictures) may mask the sinfulness, but the reality remains; from birth all of us are sinful and in need of Christ to rescue us and sustain us.

What Surrender Looks Like

A surrendered heart owns the sin without looking around for others to blame. A surrendered heart offers the sin to the Lord for Him to take away instead of offering something in an attempt to make things right. And a surrendered heart expresses no confidence in an ability to stand apart from God's grace. Instead, here is what a surrendered heart looks like:

> The sacrifice pleasing to God is a broken spirit.
> You will not despise a broken and humbled heart,
>> God. (Ps. 51:17)

David was broken before God because he knew how sinful he was in light of God's holiness. And he was broken because he knew that God's grace and forgiveness was even greater than his sin. The kindness and mercy of God breaks us when we realize it is for us. It is the kindness of God that leads us to repentance.

When we are broken before Him, He makes us whole. When we offer our sin, He takes it away. When we humble ourselves, He lifts us up.

He despises the proud, but gives grace to the humble. And it takes humility to stop blaming others, humility to quit thinking you can make things right with some sacrifice, and humility to cease your self-belief.

| THE **IMPLOSION** 2 Samuel 11 | THE **CONFRONTATION** 2 Samuel 12 | THE **CONFESSION** Psalm 51 | THE **CELEBRATION** Psalm 32 |

Psalm 32

Of David. A *Maskil.*

How joyful is the one
whose transgression is forgiven,
whose sin is covered!
How joyful is a person whom
the LORD does not charge with iniquity
and in whose spirit is no deceit!

When I kept silent, my bones became brittle
from my groaning all day long.
For day and night your hand was heavy on me;
my strength was drained
as in the summer's heat. *Selah*

Then I acknowledged my sin to you
and did not conceal my iniquity.
I said,
"I will confess my transgressions to the LORD,"
and you forgave the guilt of my sin. *Selah*

Therefore let everyone who is faithful pray to you
    immediately,
When great floodwaters come,
they will not reach him.

You are my hiding place;

you protect me from trouble.

You surround me with joyful shouts of deliverance.

   Selah

I will instruct you and show you the way to go;

with my eye on you, I will give counsel.

Do not be like a horse or mule,

without understanding,

that must be controlled with bit and bridle

or else it will not come near you.

Many pains come to the wicked,

but the one who trusts in the LORD

will have faithful love surrounding him.

Be glad in the LORD and rejoice,

you righteous ones;

shout for joy,

all you upright in heart.

Chapter Eight

Rejoice

God has thrown our sin into the sea of forgetfulness,
and has posted a sign that says, "No fishing allowed."
— *Corrie ten Boom*

In early 2014 Hiroo Onoda, a Japanese war hero who fought in World War II, died. His story is legendary and fascinating. In February 1945, opposing military landed where Onoda was stationed. Most of his fellow soldiers were killed or surrendered, but Onoda fled with three other soldiers into the jungle. He would not emerge for twenty-nine years!

Onoda continued hiding because he thought the war was still going on, though in reality it ended just a few months after he had fled into hiding. In October 1945, Hiroo and his companions saw a leaflet announcing that Japan had surrendered, but they ignored it because they deemed it as untrustworthy propaganda. More leaflets were dropped from airplanes toward the end of 1945, but they did not believe those either. News was announced and heralded that the war was over, that fighting could cease, but because they failed to believe the news, they kept hiding, kept striving, and kept fighting.

As the years passed, one of Onoda's companions left the others to surrender, and two were killed in shootouts with police. Only Onoda remained and for twenty-nine years, he lived on the run, lived as if the battle was still raging.

In 1974, a Japanese man who was traveling around the world looking for Lieutenant Onoda, a panda, and the Abominable Snowman (in that particular order) found him after only four days of searching. They became friends but Onoda refused to believe that the war was over unless he received orders from a superior officer. The Japanese government located his commanding officer, who made the trip into the jungle to relieve Onoda from his duty. The officer essentially told him, "Combat has ceased. It is finished." And he finally walked out of the jungle.[1]

While we have all failed, have all lost battles, have all wasted time in our wandering, Christ's victory is our victory. He has won the war for us. He has won the war for you.

We can walk out of the jungle of self-pity and guilt. On the cross Jesus yelled, "It is finished!" The sacrifice for our sins was complete, the punishment we deserved was paid in full, and our forgiveness was secured.

If we don't believe the good news that Christ has forgiven our sins, we will fight battles that don't matter and strive for things that won't satisfy. If we fail to believe the good news that our sins have been removed from us, we will work to achieve forgiveness instead of living in response to the forgiveness we have received.

After David confessed his sin in Psalm 51, he celebrated the forgiveness he received in Psalm 32. Remember, the Psalms were compiled over several hundred years and are placed by themes and not in chronological order in the book of Psalms. David's implosion is chronicled in 2 Samuel 11, the confrontation with the prophet Nathan in 2 Samuel 12, his prayer of confession in Psalm 51, and his celebration of forgiveness in Psalm 32.

Just as there are three different words used in Psalm 51 to describe the full nature of our depravity, there are three different phrases used to describe the fullness of our forgiveness in Psalm 32. Speaking about how God's grace trumps our sin in the psalm, Charles Spurgeon declared:

> Note the three words so often used to denote our disobedience: rebellion, sin, and iniquity, are the three-headed dog at the gates of hell, but our glorious Lord has silenced his barkings for ever against his own believing ones. The trinity of sin is overcome by the Trinity of heaven.[2]

God has the last word on our sin and He has removed it from us and remembers it no more. His grace is the trump card that annihilates all our sin. Psalm 32 is an exciting reminder that our sins are forgiven, and the three words that paint a picture of our forgiveness are powerful.

> How joyful is the one whose transgression is forgiven (*nasa'*), whose sin is covered (*kacah*)! How joyful is a person whom the Lord does not charge (*lo chasab*) with iniquity and in whose spirit is no deceit! (Ps. 32:1–2)

The psalm was Augustine's favorite, and he had the psalm inscribed on his wall as he was on his deathbed to remind himself that his sins were forgiven.[3] What good news to rejoice over! Your sin is forgiven, covered, and not charged against you.

The Extent of Forgiveness

Your Sin Is Forgiven

"How joyful is the one whose transgression is forgiven!" The word we translate "forgiven" is the Hebrew word *nasa'*, and it means to carry away. You once carried your sin, but the Lord has carried it away. As Christ carried the cross to His death, He carried your sin away with it.

Carrying our own sin is miserable and burdensome. Before David confessed his sin, he was plagued with the guilt and pain of carrying it. He was burdened with the regret of his choices, filled with anguish because he was not in close communion with God, and in constant worry that someone would find out the truth about him. He was not filled with peace but with sorrow and turmoil. David remembered those days, "For day and night your hand was heavy on me; my strength was drained as in the summer's heat."[4]

Part of David's misery came from the Lord. Because David belonged to God, God did not allow David to be satisfied in his sin. Once you have tasted God's goodness, other things will never satisfy you, and because God loves you He will lay His hand heavy on you to bring you back to Himself.

But in God's grace, David's misery and mourning was replaced with joy as his sin was carried away. If you have confessed your sin to Him, He has carried your sin away too. He has not placed it close to you so you can reflect on it or stare at it. He has carried it so far away that it is infinitely separated from you—as far as the east is from the west.

It takes faith in Christ to believe that our sins are carried away. Martin Luther said, "To be convinced in our hearts that we have forgiveness of sins and peace with God by grace alone is the hardest thing."[5] It is the hardest thing because we are hard-working self-achievers who want to earn our forgiveness instead of receiving it by faith. If we could earn our forgiveness then Christ died for nothing.

To not believe your sin is forgiven is to not trust what the Lord has declared to be true. To fail to believe your sins have been carried away is failure to believe Him. When my daughters continue to apologize for things I have already forgiven them for it breaks my heart because it causes me to think they doubt my love for them. For them to know I have forgiven them requires their trust. Trust Him and know the joy of your sin being carried away. No matter what you have done or have failed to do, if you have offered Him your life, you have simultaneously offered Him your sin. And He has carried your sin away.

Since Robin Williams' tragic death, many have remembered his greatest acting performances. Williams was an exceptional actor who entertained, provoked, and challenged us with his craft. We laughed, cried, and reflected. Many have pointed to a scene in the movie *Good Will Hunting* as one of his greatest.

In the scene, Will Hunting, played by Matt Damon, is sharing with Sean Maguire, played by Williams, about the horrific abuse he endured as a child at the hands of his foster father. Sean references his file and then continually repeats, "It's not your fault." Over and over again. For Will to really embrace that truth, the message has to be told to him over and over again.

Years of pain, years of putting barriers between himself and others, must be broken through. After hearing "It's not your fault" ten times, Will finally breaks down, throws himself into Sean's arms, and internalizes the message. Sean's repetition yields the intended result.

From an eternal vantage point, we are different from Will Hunting in that we are not innocent victims at the hands of a cruel and abusive father. Instead, we are the ones at fault, the ones who have committed holy treason against our loving and perfect Father. But we are like Will in that our hearts are prone to harden and wander. Our hearts are prone to attempt to fix things ourselves, not prone to trust the unconditional grace and love He offers us.

Because we have a hard time understanding and receiving God's grace, the Scriptures are incredibly repetitive about God's love and grace. There is an intentional rhythm of holy repetition as God's grace is heralded over and over again. His grace is so amazing that it never grows dull, and we need to be constantly reminded of it as our hearts harden without it. As Will Hunting needed the repetition, you need to hear over and over again that your sin is forgiven.

Your Sin Is Covered

"How joyful is the one whose sin is covered!" The word for "covered" in the original language *kacah*, means much more than a light covering; so don't think about covering your pancakes with syrup, or your bed with new bed sheets. Aunt Jemima syrup and the sheets don't completely bury what they are covering; you can still tell it is a pancake no matter how much syrup you use and the bed is still clearly a bed.

God's covering is much greater. When our sin is covered it is hidden without any possibility of finding. It is buried into oblivion and is out of sight forever. God buries it and chooses to forget where He buried it.

So stop looking for it. Stop digging in the past trying to find it. The sin of your implosion is gone because it is covered by His grace.

At first David attempted to cover his own sin. The elaborate cover-up that included the murder of Bathsheba's husband was David's stupid attempt to hide his own sin. But after being confronted he "acknowledged his sin and did not conceal his iniquity any longer." When he uncovered his sin, God covered it.

When we uncover our sin, God covers it.

We are a lot like David in our futile attempts to cover our tracks. Like a dog that treats your front yard like a bathroom, and actually believes that two kicks on the grass will cover what has transpired, we are idiots to think we can cover our own sin. The wayward spouse frantically deleting text messages to the mysterious lover cannot delete the sin. The professional who lied about his education on his resume cannot cover his tracks when the promotion years later causes the human resources department to discover there was no degree from that school.

We are not alone; humanity has always tried to cover sin and shame. When Adam and Eve, the first humans on the planet, disobeyed God and declared their way to be better than His, they suddenly realized they were naked, so they made fig leaves and covered themselves. Their fig leaves were insufficient, so God in His mercy fashioned clothes for them in the garden of Eden. Immediately after their rebellion, God made clothes for His people.[6]

The clothes God made came from the skins of an animal, which means God slaughtered an animal so that Adam and Eve could be clothed with the clothes God provided instead of the fig leaves they attempted to cover themselves with. The first sin was followed by the first sacrifice and it points to the ultimate sacrifice of Jesus for us. Because the covering of our own goodness is insufficient, Christ was slaughtered so we can be covered and clothed in His righteousness. You are not covered in your sin but in the grace of your Savior.

Your Sin Is Not Charged

"How joyful is a person the Lord does not charge with iniquity!" The phrase for "not charged" in the original language is *lo chasab*, which empathically means that there is absolutely no counting, remembering, or charging of your sin. Your sin is not charged to your account.

Your pride, lust, and materialism are completely gone from your account. Your selfishness, hatred, and bitterness are no longer charged against you. There is no record of the times you failed to be the spouse you should be, the employee or boss you know you should have been, the child you wish you had been to your parents, or the parent you wish you had been to your children. There is no record of sin on you. It has been expunged and wiped clean.

David's psalm is so significant and such a clear explanation of God's grace justifying us to stand before God that it is found in the New Testament. Centuries after David penned Psalm 32 and after Christ came into our world, the apostle Paul wrote the book of Romans. To illustrate how we are made right with God, the apostle Paul referenced the psalm that David wrote:

> Now to the one who works, pay is not credited as a gift, but as something owed. But to the one who does not work, but believes on him who declares the ungodly to be righteous, his faith is credited for righteousness. Just as David also speaks of the blessing of the person to whom God credits righteousness apart from works: Blessed are those whose lawless acts are forgiven and whose sins are covered. Blessed is the person the Lord will never charge with sin. (Rom. 4:4–8)

There are two approaches to God, two approaches to forgiveness. One is to work hard to make things right with God through our attempts and efforts. But our works don't make us right with God; actually our works only condemn us because they reveal how woefully short we fall of His perfection. No matter how many people affirm us for the good things we do, our good deeds cannot compare to Him. Our good deeds, if done in attempts to qualify us before God, only offend Him because we minimize His goodness and elevate our own. If we chose our works, we will receive what is owed to us, and we don't want to stand before God in what we are owed because all we are owed is death and destruction.

The second approach is to quit working and believe. When we quit trusting ourselves and believe on Him, He credits righteousness to us apart from our works. With His perfect righteousness on our legal account, we are made right before God.

Not only is your account emptied of all your sin, but it is also filled with all of Christ's righteousness. Not only are all your sins forgotten, but also the perfect obedience of Jesus is credited to you as if it is your perfect obedience.

How Jesus lived is how your account shows you have lived. How Jesus treated people is how your account shows you have treated people. How Jesus forgave is how your account shows you have forgiven. How Jesus obeyed the Father is how your account shows your obedience. How Jesus loved His enemies is how your account shows your love for enemies.

Jesus' sinless and pure life is your sinless and pure life.

Every illustration falls short of this staggering and glorious truth, but here is an attempt. Many basketball fans believe that Michael Jordan's greatest basketball game happened when his Chicago Bulls beat the Cleveland Cavaliers in March of 1990. Jordan's game, though not perfect, was close to it. He shot 23 of 27 from the field and scored 69 points in an overtime win.[7] On the Bulls team was a rookie named Stacey King. King missed some important free throws in the game and scored 1 point yet quirked to reporters after the game, "I will always remember this as the night that Michael Jordan and I combined to score 70 points." King was wise to get in on Jordan's offering, on what Jordan brought to the table.

We are wise to get in on Jesus' offering of Himself for us. And we did not bring even one point to the table. All that was on our spiritual account was our sin. William Temple has been credited for the reminder that "the only thing we contribute to our salvation is the sin that makes it necessary."[8] Yet Jesus took away our sin and gave us all the perfect righteousness that is in His account.

The Foolish and the Great Exchange

When we implode, we always make a foolish exchange. We exchange the greatness of God for something less than Him. Instead of pursuing Him, we pursue something that cannot quench. It is a foolish exchange, trading the truth and greatness of God for the lie that something else can satisfy.

Thankfully, there is an exchange that is greater than our foolish one, an exchange theologians have commonly called "the Great Exchange." On the cross, Jesus exchanged our sin for His righteousness. Jesus knew no sin but on the cross He became our sin. He became the porn addict, the thief, the workaholic who neglected his family, the mother who ignored her children, the wayward spouse, the man who lied and stole from his company, the addict, the self-consumed egomaniac, the greedy materialistic young professional, and the self-righteous unloving church member.

He lovingly traded our sin for His righteousness and forgiveness. Our sin was charged to Him and His perfection was charged to us. About the beauty of Psalm 32, Martin Luther wrote, "We are all sinners alike, only that the sins of the holy are not counted but covered; and the sins of the unholy are not covered but counted."[9]

How can you start over when you implode?

Rejoice! Celebrate the great exchange. It has trumped your foolish one. Rejoice that your sin has been forgiven, covered, and is no longer charged against you.

Chapter Nine

Look to Him

Although my memory's fading, I remember two things clearly: I am a great sinner and Christ is a great Savior.
— *John Newton*

For twenty years the iconic photo of Tiger Woods fist pumping after winning his first Masters championship was etched in the minds of his fans. The picture captured Tiger's personality, passion, and success, as he was the youngest golfer in history to win the Masters. But twenty years after that photograph, he was arrested for driving under the influence and his mug shot photo went viral. Two pictures taken twenty years apart show a very different Tiger Woods.

The celebrity mug shot has been called the great equalizer. In the celebrity mug shot, celebrities lose control over their image.[1] They don't dictate the lighting, the context, and they can't choose the perfect picture from the many that are taken.

173

There is just one, and that one picture is shared with the world via news outlets, online articles, and social media.

The mug shot is the great equalizer because it reminds us that we are all equally broken, equally in need of God's grace. All of us have mug shot moments.

The mug shot also points to the reality that great and mighty men and women fall. While people may look at the photos with pity, share them with friends, and think "this will never happen to me," implosions keep happening.

When David heard of Saul's implosion, he sang a song about the mighty falling and likely thought, "This will never happen to me." He learned lessons from Saul's implosion yet still imploded himself, which means I can write a book and you can read a book encouraging us to fight isolation, boredom, and pride and we can still ruin our lives.

After seeing many implosions, I know better than to say, "This will never happen to me." I know very well that it can easily happen to me, as men and women who loved the Lord and walked in integrity one day fell. The more people I see fall the more I feel frail. None of us are able to keep ourselves from falling.

If David had prayed Psalm 51 on the night of his implosion, he would not have needed to pray Psalm 51 later. He would have relied on the Lord and not himself. Or if David had sung Psalm 32, he would not have imploded. He would have been rejoicing in God's grace and forgiveness and would not have been looking with boredom from the roof of the palace.

David's posture when he turned to the Lord is the only posture that will prevent us from implosion. What David needed to avoid implosion, what we need to keep from falling, is deep dependence on the Lord. As we look to Him, isolation, boredom, and pride are defeated. As we rely on Him, we are humbled and never bored. As we follow Him, He puts us in community with others.

We need to pray Psalm 51 and Psalm 32 again and again. We need to humbly throw ourselves on His grace and rejoice in the forgiveness He has given. As we look to Him, He will keep us to Himself and keep us from falling. Only He can keep us from falling.

Years after David, another King was born in Bethlehem, the same town where David was anointed as king. Jesus, the One who the prophets wrote about and the bloody sacrifices pointed to, entered our world to rescue us from ourselves. The Gospel of Matthew opens with the lineage of King Jesus. In the lineage, we find this phrase, "Jesse fathered King David. David fathered Solomon by Uriah's wife."[2]

In the lineage of Jesus is the marriage of David and Bathsheba. David's sin was not the end. The destruction and the fallout from his sin was not the end either. From the union of David and Bathsheba came Solomon, and the sacred lineage continued all the way to Jesus. God fashioned a beautiful story from the mess David made of his life, and God can fashion a beautiful story from our ruin too.

David as an earthly king gives us a glimpse of Jesus as our King. As David defeated the enemies of God's people, Jesus defeated sin and shame for us. As David represented all of Israel as he stood before Goliath and emerged victorious, Jesus represents us. His victory over death is our victory. As David ruled over his kingdom and shepherded the people well, Jesus rules over His kingdom and shepherds us with great wisdom and compassion.

But unlike king David, Jesus Christ is the perfect King. He has never pursued impurity, has never misused His authority, and has never failed to keep His promises.

When we are weak, He is strong. When we are unfaithful, He is faithful. When we are unable to stand, He is able to keep us from falling.

> Now to him who is able to protect you from stumbling and to make you stand in the presence of his glory, without blemish and with great joy, to the only God our Savior, through Jesus Christ our Lord, be glory, majesty, power, and authority before all time, now and forever. Amen. (Jude 24–25)

Notes

Chapter One

1. 1 Timothy 3:1–7.

2. To read the lists of qualifications to lead God's church, see 1 Peter 5:1–3, 1 Timothy 3:1–12, and Titus 1:5–9.

3. 1 Timothy 5:9.

4. See the tragic end of Solomon's legacy in 1 Kings 11. Both David's fall and Solomon's drift from the Lord are in the eleventh chapter of books. It is not intentional, as the original manuscripts did not have chapters and verses in them, but it is ironic and helps me remember where the stories are in the Bible as "Chapter 11" is a phrase used in our culture to describe bankruptcy.

Chapter Two

1. Jim Collins, *Good to Great: Why Some Companies Make the Leap . . . And Others Don't* (New York: Harper Business, 2001).

2. Jim Collins, *How the Mighty Fall: And Why Some Companies Never Give In* (London: Random House Business, 2009).

3. In 2 Samuel 23:8–39, there is a list of David's mighty men.

4. In 1 Samuel 13:14, we see David called a "man after God's own heart."

5. In 2 Samuel 6, David leads Israel in celebration as the ark of the covenant is brought into Jerusalem. David dances and takes off his outer garment, which Michal, daughter of Saul, chastised him for doing. David insisted he would become even more undignified, that he did not care how he looked, that he would celebrate before the Lord. Saul, on the other hand, was consumed with his own image.

6. To read the account of God giving the people a king, see 1 Samuel 8:18–22. The account of Saul being anointed as king is in 1 Samuel 9. The account of his suicide is in 1 Samuel 31.

7. First Samuel 16 gives us the account of David being anointed as future king because "God looks at the heart while man looks at the outward appearance."

8. First Samuel 18 gives a picture of Saul's despair, David's skillful artistry and warrior ways, as well as the story of the two hundred foreskins.

9. Several chapters in the Bible, 1 Samuel 19–24, chronicle David's life on the run from Saul. Saul, as king, wasted incredible time, resources, and energy pursuing to kill the man who fought for him, played for him, and served the people well.

10. The promise to David can be found in 2 Samuel 7.

11. 2 Samuel 10:19.

12. 2 Samuel 11:15.

13. 2 Samuel 11:27.

14. Nathan's confrontation of David is in 2 Samuel 12.

15. 2 Samuel 12:6.

16. 2 Samuel 12:7.

17. See 2 Samuel 18 to read the account of David's son, Absalom, death.

18. cf. 2 Samuel 16:10.

19. In 2 Samuel 2, David sang a song lamenting Saul's death. Twice in the song he used the phrase, "How the Mighty Have Fallen."

Chapter Three

1. "Ten Years of 'If You See Something, Say Something,'" March 19, 2012, accessed October 6, 2017, http://reason.com/blog/2012/03/19/ten-years-of-if-you-see-something-say-so.

2. The Lord's instructions for how a census should be taken can be found in Exodus 30:11–16, and Joab's rebuke to David and his refusal to carry out the full census is found in 1 Chronicles 21. Just as David's sin with Bathsheba brought the Lord's discipline, so did the census as seventy thousand people died because of a famine. We see in David's life and throughout the Old Testament that God's holiness demands that sin be punished. The good news for us is that Christ took all our punishment for us on the cross where He died in our place.

3. 2 Samuel 19:5.

4. R. D. Putman, *Bowling Alone: The Collapse and Revival of American Community* (New York: Simon & Schuster, 2000).

5. Associated Press, "Ventura Says Religion Is For 'Weak,'" *New York Times*, October 1, 1999, http://www.nytimes.com/1999/10/01/us/ventura-says-religion-is-for-weak.html.

6. Todd Spangler, "Binge Boom: Young U.S. Viewers Gulp Down Average of Six TV Episodes Per Sitting," *Variety*, March 21, 2017, http://variety.com/2017/digital/news/ binge-viewing -tv-survey-millennials-1202013560/.

7. International Communication Association, "Feelings of Loneliness and Depression Linked to Binge-Watching Television," January 29, 2015, https://www.eurekalert.org/ pub_ releases/2015-01/ica-fol012615.php.

8. Eric Geiger and Ed Stetzer, *Transformational Groups: Creating a New Scorecard for Groups* (Nashville: B&H Publishing Group, 2014).

9. Hebrews 3:13.

10. Hebrews 3:13 reminds us that community keeps our hearts from hardening. In Philippians 1:6, The apostle Paul expressed his confidence that believers living in the city of Philippi would continue in the faith, that God would continue His gracious work in them. One of the reasons for Paul's confidence was his belief in the power of Christian community, that these believers enjoyed a "partnership in the gospel" (Phil. 1:5). Their partnership in the gospel is what gave Paul the confidence that they would continue.

11. Association for Psychological Science, "Darkness Increases Dishonest Behavior, "news release, March 1, 2010, https://www .psychologicalscience.org/media/releases/ 2010/zhong.cfm.

12. Dietrich Bonhoeffer, *Life Together* (London: SCM Press, 1954), chapter 5.

13. John, one of Jesus' disciples, recorded Jesus' invitation to walk in the light (John 8:12), and when John later wrote to believers he encouraged them that they have fellowship with one another

as they walk in the light (I John 1:7). There is a deep connection between the fellowship with other believers and obedience.

14. Hal Niedzviecki, "Facebook in a Crowd," *New York Times*, October 24, 2008, http://www.nytimes.com/2008/10/26/magazine/26lives-t.html?_r=0.

15. Deborah Hastings, "Illinois Woman Found Dead at Home Had Died More Than a Year Earlier," *New York Daily News*, January 1, 2015, http://www.nydailynews.com/news/ national/illinois-woman-found-dead-home-year-dying-article-1.2063017.

16. As examples, the word *koinonia* is translated "fellowship" in Acts 2:42. The early believers committed themselves to the fellowship, to caring for one another. The word is translated "partnership" in Philippians 1:5, as the believers living in Philippi were partners together in the gospel.

17. Mark Oppenheimer, "When Some Turn To Church, Others Go to CrossFit," *New York Times*, November 27, 2015, https://www.nytimes.com/2015/11/28/us/some-turn-to-church-others-to-crossfit.html?_r=0.

18. David Sax, *Revenge of Analog: Real Things and Why They Matter* (New York: Public Affairs, 2016).

19. *Saint Augustine of Hippo Collection* (Aeterna Press, 2016).

Chapter Four

1. Judy Wills, "Neuroscience Reveals That Boredom Hurts," *Phi Delta Kappan* 95, no. 8 (2014): 28–32, http://journals.sagepub.com/doi/abs/10.1177/003172171409500807? journalCode=pdka&.

2. Kevin Conlon, "'Bored' Oklahoma Teen Convicted in Random 'Thrill Kill,'" *CNN*, April 18, 2015, http://www.cnn.com /2015/04/18/us/thrill-kill-teen-convicted/.

3. "German Nurse 'Sorry' for Killing Patients," *BBC*, February 19, 2015, http://www.bbc.com/ news/ world-europe-31532875.

4. Psalm 57:1.

5. Psalm 34:5.

6. Psalm 52:7.

7. Psalm 52:9.

8. Blaise Pascal, *Pensées*, rev. ed. (London: Penguin, 1995).

9. Megan McCluskey, "Instagram Star Essena O'Neill Breaks Her Silence on Quitting Social Media," *TIME*, January 5, 2016, http://time.com/4167856/essena-oneill-breaks-silence-on-quitting-social-media/.

10. Stephanie Land, "I Spent 2 Years Cleaning Houses. What I Saw Makes Me Never Want to Be Rich," *Vox*, November 12, 2015, http://www.vox.com/2015/7/16/8961799/ housekeeper-job-clients.

11. Kirsten Weir, "Never a Dull Moment: Things Get Interesting When Psychologists Take a Closer Look at Boredom," *Monitor on Psychology* 44, no. 7 (2013): 54, http://www.apa.org/monitor /2013/07-08/dull-moment.aspx.

12. Augustine, *Confessions, Vol. 1* (Oxford Press, 2013).

13. C. S. Lewis, *Mere Christianity* (San Francisco: Harper Collins, 2001), 136–37.

14. Jeremiah 2:12–13.

15. In one of his classic sermons, "The Excellency of Christ," Jonathan Edwards declared "so great is he, that all men, all kings

and princes, are as worms of the dust before him; all nations are as the drop of the bucket, and the light dust of the balance; yea, and angels themselves are as nothing before him. He is so high, that he is infinitely above any need of us; above our reach, that we cannot be profitable to him; and above our conceptions, that we cannot comprehend him." See http://www.ccel.org/ccel/ edwards/sermons. excellency.html.

16. Jared Wilson, *Gospel Deeps: Reveling in the Excellencies of Jesus* (Chicago: Crossway, 2012), 80–81.

17. Jeremiah 2:25.

18. Hosea 1–2.

19. Augustine, *Confessions, Vol. 6* (Oxford: Oxford University Press, 2013).

20. For a video of the interview, go here: https://www.you tube.com/watch ?v=4HeLYQaZQW0.

21. Helen Lemmel, "Turn Your Eyes Upon Jesus," 1922, first published in *Glad Songs* by the British National Sunday School Union.

Chapter Five

1. To see the odds of making it from playing sports in high school to college to professionally, the NCAA offers these statistics: http:// www.ncaa.org/about/resources/research/probability-competing -beyond-high-school

2. Pablo Torre, "Why and How Athletes Go Broke," *Sports Illustrated*, March 23, 2009, https://www.si.com/vault/2009/ 03/23/105789480/how-and-why-athletes-go-broke.

3. Bob Wolfey, "ESPN Films Documentary Explores Why Some Athletes Go Broke," *Milwaukee Journal Sentinel*, September 30, 2012, http://archive.jsonline.com/blogs/ sports/171925931.html.

4. Robert Pagliarini, "Why Athletes Go Broke (It's Not What You Think)," *Huffington Post*, July 2, 2013, http://www.huffington-post.com/robert-pagliarini/why-athletes-go-broke_b_3526378.html.

5. Skip Prichard, "The Power of Executive Candor," Rittenhouse Rankings, October 28, 2013, http://www.rittenhouserankings.com/the-power-of-executive-candor/.

6. See Psalm 57.

7. The phrase that pride causes us to see great things as less than they are comes from Jon Bloom's excellent article, "Don't Let Pride Steal Your Joy," Desiring God, May 8, 2015, http://www.desiringgod.org/articles/don-t-let-pride-steal-your-joy.

8. 1 Peter 5:8.

9. Ezekiel 28 is a chapter in the Bible that is about a wicked king of Tyre but also about Satan. Verses 14–18 recount Satan's fall. He was a created angel of God, and his heart became proud because of his beauty. Isaiah 14 is similar in that is recounts the fall of Satan. In this chapter we see that Satan was expelled from heaven because he wanted to be like God, equal with God.

10. D. A. Carson, *The God Who is There: Finding Your Place in God's Story* (Grand Rapids: Baker, 2010), 32.

11. Lewis, *Mere Christianity*, 123–24.

12. Charles Duhigg, *The Power of Habit: Why We Do What We Do In Life and Business* (New York: Random House, 2014), 55.

13. God commanded Saul to wait for the prophet Samuel to offer sacrifices (see 1 Sam. 10:8), but Saul did not want to wait, believed he could override the Lord's command, and offered sacrifices himself (see 1 Sam. 13:13).

14. 1 Samuel 15:1–9.

15. 2 Chronicles 26:16.

16. 2 Chronicles 26:4.

17. John Owen, *The Mortification of Sin*, chapter 2.

18. Lewis, *Mere Christianity*, 128.

19. Andrew Murray, *Humility*, Legacy of Faith Library (Nashville: B&H Publishing Group, 2017).

20. The first of Martin Luther's *95 Theses* is: "When our Lord and Master Jesus Christ said, 'Repent' (Mt 4:17), he willed the entire life of believers to be one of repentance." Martin Luther, *Martin Luther*, Legacy of Faith Library (Nashville: B&H Publishing Group, 2017).

Chapter Six

1. Luke 15:11–32.

2. 2 Samuel 12:13.

3. The story of God commanding Saul to destroy the Amalekites is in 1 Samuel 15. It is a challenging and difficulty story to read because God asked Saul to destroy all the people. How do we reconcile this command with the truth that God is love? Here is what we know: the Amalekites attacked God's people, Israel, hundreds of years earlier when the Israelites left Egyptian slavery. God promised His people that He would wipe out Amalek, as God has always promised to bless those who bless His people and

curse those who curse His people. The story reminds us that God has a special protective love for His own. It is good to belong to God. Years after Saul disobeyed, the Amalekites attached Israel. During David's reign the Amalekites attacked and kidnapped the wives and children of David's men (1 Samuel 30).

4. Matthew 15:19.

5. Michael Greger, *How Not to Die: Discover the Foods Scientifically Proven to Prevent and Reverse Disease* (New York: Flatiron, 2015), 17.

6. *Praying the Psalms with Luther* (St. Louis: Concordia, 2007), 124.

7. Tim Keller, *Gospel Christianity: Participant's Guide* (New York: Redeemer Presbyterian Church, 2007), 14.

8. Isaiah 64:6.

9. Mark 2:17.

10. Mark 8:34.

11. 2 Corinthians 5:17.

12. John 3:3, 14–15.

13. Victor Hugo, *Les Misérables*, trans. Charles E. Wilbour (New York: Random House Modern Library, 1992).

14. 1 Peter 1:18–19.

15. Luke 7:36–50.

16. If you are unfamiliar with the event . . . at the 2017 Oscars, the movie *La La Land* was announced as winning the coveted Best Picture. But when *La La Land*'s producer received the envelope, and saw that the real winner was *Moonlight*, he stepped forward and declared, "This is not a joke. *Moonlight* is the real winner." People quickly looked for someone to blame.

17. J. I. Packer, *Knowing God* (Downers Grove: InterVarsity, 1973), 161–66.

Chapter Seven

1. 2 Corinthians 5:21.

2. Just as "justified" is a legal term declaring one is made right in the eyes of the law, "condemnation" is a legal term declaring one is guilty and will pay the price for the guilt. Romans 8:1 beautifully teaches that "there is now no condemnation for those in Christ." There is no condemnation for believers because God "condemned sin in the flesh by sending his own Son in the likeness of sinful flesh as a sin offering" (Rom. 8:4). The book of Romans also teaches us that God restrained His wrath and passed over the sins previously committed, the sins committed before Christ, because Christ would bear the punishment (Rom. 3:24). David was forgiven because of Christ just as we are forgiven because of Christ.

3. Because Christ received the punishment, theologians emphasize that what happened to David was "discipline" and not "punishment." For example, see: John Piper, "Consequences of Forgiven Sin," in *A Godward Life: Savoring the Supremacy of God in All of Life* (Colorado Springs: Multnomah, 2015), 237.

4. Psalm 51:3–4.

5. 1 Samuel 15:24.

6. 1 Kings 15:22.

7. Daniel Effron has researched and written about moral licensing. For more, see: https://www.danieleffron.com/overview.

8. Psalm 51:12a.

9. Psalm 51:12b.

Chapter Eight

1. Robert McFadden, "Hiroo Onoda, Whose War Lasted Decades, Dies at 91," *New York Times*, January 18, 2014, A21.

2. Charles Spurgeon, *The Treasury of David*, vol. 1 (Nashville: Thomas Nelson, 1984), 82.

3. James Montgomery Boice, *Psalms*, vol. 1 (Grand Rapids: Baker, 1994), 277.

4. Psalm 32:4.

5. Martin Luther, *Commentary on Galatians* (North Charleston: CreateSpace Independent Publishing Platform, 2012).

6. Genesis 3:21.

7. Associated Press, "Among Jordan's Great Games, This Was It," *Los Angeles Times*, March 29, 1990, http://articles.latimes.com/1990-03-29/sports/sp-582_1_michael-jordan.

8. William Temple is commonly credited with the statement although others have also credited Jonathan Edwards with the quote. Regardless, it is beautiful and true.

9. *Praying the Psalms with Luther* (St. Louis: Concordia, 2007).

Chapter Nine

1. Travis M. Andrews, "The Mug Shot is 'The Great Equalizer.' Just Look at Tiger Woods," *The Washington Post*, May 30, 2017, https://www.washingtonpost.com/news /morning-mix/wp/2017/05/30/the-mugshot-is-the-great-equalizer-just-look-at-tiger-woods/?utm_term=.e50bdb92ccf8.

2. Matthew 1:6.